Network Now

English

B1.1

Teacher's Book

Lynda Hübner

Klett-Langenscheidt

München

Network Now B1.1 – Teacher's Book

Autorin:
Lynda Hübner

Redaktion:
Helge Sturmfels (Projektleitung)
Kirsten Mannich

Satz und Layout:
kaltner verlagsmedien GmbH, Bobingen

Umschlagkonzept:
Design im Kontor – Iris Steiner, Kassel

Fotos:
Cover photograph: shutterstock / Leigh Richardson (main picture – Durdle Door, Dorset),
Riccardo Piccinini

Lehrwerkskomponenten:	
Student's Book mit 3 Audio-CDs	605122
Teacher's Book	605123

www.klett-langenscheidt.de/networknow

1. Auflage   1 ⁵ ⁴ ³ ² ¹ | 2017 16 15 14 13

Gesamtherstellung: Print Consult GmbH, München

ISBN 978-3-12-605123-1

MIX
Papier aus verantwor-
tungsvollen Quellen
FSC® C084279

Contents

Contents

Welcome

Welcome to the *Teacher's Book* for *Network Now B1.1*

Your course: *Network Now B1.1*

- *Network Now B1.1* provides 24 ninety-minute lessons, for a 2-semester course.
- Each of the 6 units has 3 steps (18 lessons), followed by a revision lesson, *Now I can* (6 lessons).
- If your course has more than 24 lessons and you need **extra lessons**, you can use the 3 optional pages at the end of each unit: *English worldwide* (page 28), *English at work* (page 29) and *Story* (page 30) or *Playing with English* (page 52). Each of the 18 pages provides approximately 30 minutes of classroom material, a total of 6 extra lessons.

Your *Network Now B1.1* coursebook

- The **Photo page** (page 9) at the start of each unit has topic-related photos and a brief task. Allow students a few minutes to look at this and to read the listed aims of the unit.
- All lessons begin with a five-minute *Starter* activity to lead into the topic.
- If an activity involves a **listening** exercise, the track numbers are given with the relevant activities: $\circledcirc_{2/13}$ = CD number 2, track 13.
- In **Steps 1 and 2**, you'll often find elements of 'refresher' grammar (*You already know*) before the new grammar (*And now*) is introduced (pages 15 + 16).
- There are *Now you* exercises (page 12) in each step, allowing students to speak about their own experiences and opinions.
- The final activity in Steps 1, 2 and 3 is *What do you think?* (page 17). Photos and quotations prompt students to talk in groups or in class about topic-related themes.
- Remind the class that at the end of Steps 1 and 2, there's a *Language study* page which explains and practises the grammar, and a *Selfstudy* page with assorted exercises based on the unit content (pages 13/14). Refer them to the **online codes** next to the *Language study* and *Selfstudy* headings so that they have the option to do the exercises online. And, by clicking on *Need more practice?*, learners can 'backtrack' and access *Language study* exercises, on the same structure, from earlier *Network* books.
- **Step 3** (pages 20 ff.) of each unit has a focus on realia, reading and vocabulary and has just a minor grammar element. The one-page Selfstudy (page 23) has a section on *Dictionary skills*.
- The fourth lesson in the unit, *Now I can*, is a review lesson which mirrors the learning aims on the Photo page. There's a *Now you choose* activity where students can choose whether they want to try an easy *, standard ** or challenging *** task.
- The homework section after *Now I can* is a 2-page *Test yourself*, based on the exercise formats of the *telc* English B1 and *PET* exams.
- Students can find an **alphabetical dictionary** and a **unit-by-unit wordlist online** – see **www.klett-langenscheidt.de/networknow/vocabulary**.

Your *Network Now B1.1 Teacher's Book*

- This book provides **teaching notes, audio scripts, keys, tips** and **extra activities** for each step, plus ideas on using the optional pages at the end of each unit.
- If you see information in the teacher's notes in grey, it means this stage is **optional**.
- Suggestions are made on how to make some exercises simpler ($\downarrow$) or more complex ($\uparrow$) for the class. Some activities offer the students a **choice of complexity**. The one-star * option is slightly easier than the standard, two-star ** option, and the three-star *** option is more challenging.
- If you want to use **extra materials**, you can download an extra activity for each step from the Internet – but you'll need to allow extra time for these – see **www.klett-langenscheidt.de/networknow/activities**. You can also download other extra materials (e.g. Christmas activities) from here (see "Weitere Activities").
- On pages 61–64, there are photocopiable *Conversation springboards*, free-speaking activities designed to last about 20 minutes each.

So all it remains for the *Network* team to say is: Enjoy your teaching with *Network Now B1.1*.

Unit 1 Step 1 Good neighbours

Contents

Text topic A magazine article about ex-partners living next door to each other
Functions Talking about relationships; Describing someone's personality
Vocabulary Personality
Grammar **You already know:** Review of tenses (present simple, past simple, present perfect)

Lesson notes

www Extra activity: www.klett-langenscheidt.de/networknow/activities (Unit 1: Step 1)

Starter 5– mins • Ask individual students the *Starter* questions.

Text **I live next door to my ex!** 5 mins
• Board: Where do they all live? (in Sweden), How many children do they have? (three in total).
Students read the text. Check the answers in class.

Tip: Reading skills (1) The comprehension questions at this level are more complex and demanding, requiring students to pick out several aspects and bring them together in a mini-summary. Encourage students to underline the key points in the text before formulating an answer.

1a **A good divorce** 10 mins

• Give students time to read the comprehension questions and underline key information in the text.
1 They were married but now they're divorced. 2 She likes: he's a good father, he's very reliable, he's generous. She dislikes: he's a total control freak, he's so tidy. 3 He likes: she's a great mum, she's very patient, she's always cheerful, she's very creative and spontaneous. He dislikes: her house is always total chaos, her half-finished projects are everywhere. 4 They have a lot of contact. 5 Possible answer: It works well because they have a good relationship, they're both happy in their new relationships and it means their children can see both of them regularly.

1b **Talk about it** 5 mins
• Students talk together in class or in groups.

2a **Vocabulary: Personality** 10 mins
• Read out the first instruction and the words to the class. Students match a word to a statement.

1 generous, 2 honest, 3 reliable, 4 confident, 5 cheerful, 6 independent, 7 tidy, 8 spontaneous, 9 patient, 10 shy
• Students listen and check their answers. Play ▶ 1/2.
• Students listen and repeat the words in chorus. Play ▶ 1/3.

(S1 = speaker 1, S2 = speaker 2)	S1: I can manage everything by myself.
S1: I like giving.	S2: She's independent.
S2: She's generous.	S1: I like to keep everything in its place.
S1: I always tell the truth.	S2: She's tidy.
S2: She's honest.	S1: I don't plan, but I make quick decisions.
S1: You can count on me!	S2: She's spontaneous.
S2: She's reliable.	S1: I don't get angry if things take a long time.
S1: I feel sure of my own abilities.	S2: She's patient.
S2: She's confident.	S1: I don't feel comfortable in big groups or with
S1: I always smile and look happy.	new people.
S2: She's cheerful.	S2: She's shy.

I'm generous. I'm honest. I'm reliable. I'm confident. I'm cheerful. I'm incependent. I'm tidy. I'm spontaneous. I'm patient. I'm shy.

2b   **Now you: Your personality**   10 mins
NB The *Now you* exercises allow students to personalise the language items they have just learnt.

3a   **Look again**   5 mins

Tip: Task complexity (1) When you see an arrow like this ↓ , there's a suggestion how to make the activity a little easier. When you see this arrow ↑ , there's a suggestion how to make the activity a bit more demanding.

- ↓ Board: a) I went to Berlin yesterday.   b) I've been a teacher for five years.   c) I live in London.
  Read out the three facts about the tenses (1, 2, 3). Ask students to match them to the sentences (a), b), c)) on the board. (a) 2, b) 3, c) 1)
- Follow coursebook instructions.
  1 I live in the suburbs. My husband lives next door. Karl's a good father. We have a good relationship. This arrangement works well. We're both happy. Etc. 2 Karl and I got divorced. They stayed with me. I met and married my second husband and moved into his house. I heard that the house next door was for sale. They moved in. Etc. 3 One couple have taken this to the extreme. We've both tried to put the children's needs first. We've been divorced for a long time. Lena's always been a great mum. Etc.

3b   **Grammar: You already know – Review of tenses**   5 mins
! If you want to spend longer on the grammar, look at the Language study on page 13.

If short of time
- Do *Exercise 3c* as a class activity.
- In *Exercise 6*, get students to talk about just one of the topics in class.

3c   **Now you: Your living arrangements**   5 mins

Extra

Review of tenses   10 mins
• On a piece of paper with their name on, students complete the sentences from *Exercise 3c*.   • The papers are collected and then randomly given out again.   • Individuals read out the information: *He / She lives* … and the class guesses who the student is.

4   **Life Swap**   10 mins
- Read out the first instruction and play ▶ 1/4.

  Woman 1: We live together and work together. Woman 2: We're married but we don't live together.
- Read out the second instruction. Allow time for the students to read the questions, then play ▶ 1/5.
  1 a) They design and sell baby clothes. b) They've had their business for four years. c) They have similar personalities. 2 a) They've been married about five years. b) Other people think it's unnatural or think that they don't get on well. c) No, they didn't.

(P = presenter, W1 = wife 1, W2 = wife 2)   P: In this week's *Life Swap*, two people with very different lifestyles change places for a week. This week, it's two women who are going to swap places – and swap husbands. First, let's meet them. Here's tonight's first life swapper: W1:   My husband and I have a business together. We design and sell baby clothes and accessories. We started the company when our daughter was about six months old and I couldn't find any nice clothes for her – well, nothing I liked anyway. In one way it's good because we can work from home a lot of the time and we can both look after our daughter. She's four and a half now, so she'll be at school full-time next year and then we'll have more time for the business. My husband and I get on very well together and we have quite similar personalities, but, yes, of course, sometimes we have arguments about the business, but, no, usually it's OK.   P: And here's the person who she's going to swap places with: W2:   My husband and I have been together for about ten years and we've been married for about half of that time. But we don't share a house. I know people think that it's unnatural, or that we don't get on well, but it works for us. He has a really nice house, which is also his clinic – he's a therapist. And I like my flat. It's near my work and, I don't know, I just like it. We're both quite independent people, and we each have our own interests and our own friends, so it works well for us. We spend two or three nights together a week, and when we do, it's special. It's a bit like a date. I have clothes and a toothbrush at his house, and he has a few things at mine, but basically we live separately. We didn't really plan it like that, it just sort of happened.   P: Now let's meet their husbands and find out what life is like at home at the moment.

5a　**How to talk about relationships**　5 mins
* Read out the phrases and have the class repeat them in chorus.

5b　**Now you choose: Relationships**　5+ mins
* Students choose which task they'd like to do. Everyone who choose *Free time* stands up and finds a partner. Then the *Work* group get into pairs.
* Students talk to their partners. Monitor and help where needed.

6　**What do you think?** 5+ mins　5+ mins
* Students work in groups of 3 or 4 and give their opinions on the topics.

Unit 1 Step 2 At home with animals

Contents

Text topic An email extract about a crocodile zoo
Functions Describing a visit
Vocabulary Pets and wild animals
Grammar **You already know:** Present simple and present progressive
And now: Present simple to express states

Lesson notes

www　**Extra activity:** www.klett-langenscheidt.de/networknow/activities (Unit 1: Step 2)

Info　Your students can 'visit' Shaun Foggett's zoo online by typing his name into their search engine.

Starter　5 mins　• Ask individual students the *Starter* question and get them to give their reasons.

Tip: Setting up listening activities (1) It's important to set up listening activities by clearly reading out the instructions and then giving students time to read the statements or questions.

1a　**A man and his pets**　10 mins
* Students read the statements, listen, and note down one fact in each category. Play ▶ 1/10.
* ↓ Students note down facts for 1 and 3. Play ▶ 1/10.
* Check answers in class and repeat for the second part. Play ▶ 1/11.
Possible answers: **1 It's in Oxfordshire / Witney. / It's a normal family house. / It has a garden. 2 He has a fiancée. / He has two children. 3 He has 24 crocodiles. / They live in their own building in the garden. / He checks on them twice a day. 4 He hopes to open a crocodile zoo. / He hopes to get a bank loan for it.**

> (P = radio presenter, R = reporter)
> P: Next on 'Out and About in Oxfordshire', we're going over to Dave, our reporter, who's out and about somewhere in the local area. Where are you this afternoon, Dave?
> R: Hi there! Yes, I'm out and about. I'm in Witney and I'm in a garden. It's the back garden of a very nice, very normal, family house.
> P: Whose house is it?
> R: The house belongs to a man called Shaun Foggett and Shaun lives here with his fiancée Lisa, their two children ... and Shaun's pets.
> P: OK, and why are you in the back garden, not at the front door?
> R: Good question. I'm standing outside the door of a small building here at the end of the garden. It's a sort of garage and it's here that Shaun's pets live.
> P: Right, now, if they have to live in their own building at the end of the garden, then I guess we aren't talking here about a couple of hamsters or a rabbit.
> R: No, you're right. Shaun has 24 crocodiles. His collection includes three of the most endangered reptiles in the world – Chinese alligators, Siamese Crocodiles and Cuban crocodiles. He also has two black

caiman crocodiles. Shaun is passionate about these animals and about their conservation. In fact, he wants to open the first crocodile zoo in the UK and he's doing his best to make it happen. He's looking for a suitable place in the local area and he's waiting to hear from the bank about a loan.

P: I should think the bank might be a bit nervous about that idea.

R: That's the problem. He and his fiancée may have to sell their family home to make his dream come true.

P: But 24 crocodiles? In his garden? Isn't that a bit dangerous? What do the neighbours think?

R: Shaun takes safety very seriously. All of his reptiles are kept safely in this building. He checks them twice a day. There's a big lock on the door and his children aren't allowed in. Only Shaun and Lisa are allowed in. They're both in there now, in fact. I can tell you what's happening because I can see through the window. Shaun is cleaning out one of the tanks and Lisa is helping. Shaun is taking a crocodile out of its tank and ... oh, I see, Lisa is putting sticky tape around the animal's mouth – or is it its nose? – well, around its jaws – to keep those jaws closed and to keep those teeth out of the way. I must say – I'm very impressed with their professional handling of these dangerous animals.

P: So, are you going in then, Dave?

R: Right, here I go. Wish me luck ...

2a Look again 5 mins
2 (general fact), 1 (happening now), 3 (Shaun is in the middle of doing)

2b Grammar: You already know – Present simple and present progressive 5– mins
• Focus attention on the Grammar box and ask: *Which sentence is happening now?* (... is cleaning out one of the tanks.), *Which two sentences are general facts?* (... takes ... / ... checks ...), *Which one shows Shaun is in the middle of doing something?* (He's looking ...).
! For more explanations and practice, you can look at the Language study on page 18.

2c Shaun's family 5 mins
1 works, 2 is cutting, 3 have, 4 go, 5 are preparing, 6 is expecting

2d Now you: Your life 5+ mins
• ↓ Write three sentences about yourself as a pattern on the board.

3 Text A day out 10– mins

Tip: Reading skills (2) It helps to set a context for a text before students read it. You can do this by asking students to speculate about the pictures, or read the text title and say what they think the text is about, or give them key words and ask what the text might be about.

• ↓ Tell students life has moved on for Shaun. Write the key words on the board and ask the class what they think has happened to Shaun. Board: zoo – crocodiles and snakes – TV series (He has his own zoo which has crocodiles and snakes in it and he has his own TV series.)
• Give students time to read the text and then ask and answer the questions in class.

Tip: Task complexity (2) Some exercises have a star system which allows all the class to do the same basic exercise, but to varying degrees of complexity – they can choose if they want to try a simple task *, a standard task ** or a more complex task ***.

• Board: * Answer number 1 only.
** As in the coursebook.
*** As in coursebook and then write one follow-up question to ask the class.
1 He has made his dream come true. He now owns his own zoo.
2 The chance to feed and handle some of the reptiles.

4a Grammar: And now – Present simple to express states 5 mins
• Look at the Grammar box. Tell the class that these verbs aren't usually used in the progressive form.
! For more explanations and practice, you can look at the Language study on page 18.
NB Some verbs can take both forms: *He's looking out of the window* (an activity that you can start and stop at will). *He looks cold* (a state). *He's having breakfast. He has grey hair.* This needn't be brought into the lesson unless a student asks a specific question about it.

4b Find them 5 mins
belongs, owns, wants, understands, knows, has, have, is, seem, don't smell

Extra

> **Present simple to express states**   10 mins
> - Give positive and negative prompts and let a volunteer make a sentence about him- / herself.
>   Board: I (don't) understand …, I know …, I feel …, I think that …, I want …, I need …, I have …, I like …

4c   **Live from the zoo**   5 mins
- Students do the exercise, then compare answers with a partner before checking in class.
  1 am ('m) talking, 2 are sitting, 3 look, 4 are ('re) holding, 5 belongs, 6 is ('s) eating, 7 don't understand, 8 doesn't seem

5   **Vocabulary: Wild animals**   5 mins
- Play ▶ 1/12. Students listen and repeat in chorus before doing the task.

6a   **How to describe a visit**   10 mins
- Read out the phrases and ask individuals to use at least two of the phrases to describe a visit they went on.

If short of time
- Do *Exercise 6b* for homework (and then display the tasks in class in the next lesson).

6b   **Now you choose: A visit**   5+ mins
- Ask students to choose a task to do. When they've finished, they read it to someone who chose the same one.

7   **What do you think?**   5+ mins
- Class or group discussion prompted by photos. If necessary, give prompt words: *zoo, safari, circus.*

Unit 1 Step 3 House swapping

Contents

Text topic   An advertisement for a flat to rent
Functions   Talking about accommodation
Vocabulary   Abbreviations in property ads; Accommodation; Compound adjectives (a two-room flat)
Grammar   Focus on: *for / ago*
Reading   Free holiday?

Lesson notes   NB The main focus of Step 3 is vocabulary extension and reading skills.

www   Extra activity: www.klett-langenscheidt.de/networknow/activities (Unit 1: Step 3)

Starter   5 mins • Ask individual students the *Starter* questions and encourage questions from the class.

1a   **Close-up: Rental ads**   5+ mins

Tip: Realia (1) In each Step 3, there's a magnified element of realia and you can add to this by bringing your own collection of authentic materials to the lesson. You can also use German materials if you can't find what you want in English. For example, you can bring in accommodation ads from a local paper and get students to give the gist of the content in English, reminding them *not* to translate every word, but to get the general idea across to someone. Good practice in mediation!

Possible answers: **It's in Salford, in Manchester. It's on the third floor. It's got two bedrooms, a living room, kitchen, bathroom and a balcony. There's access to the garden and parking. It's near the city centre. It costs £850 per month + bills. You can move in on the 1st of February.**

1b   **Abbreviations**   5 mins
per calendar month, week, renovated building, ground floor, inclusive, street, road

2a   **Places to live**   5 mins
- Follow coursebook instructions.

2b   **Types of accommodation**   5 mins
- Read out the list of accommodation and have students repeat the words in chorus.
- In class, students match the words to the pictures.
- Ask individuals which home they would like to live in.

    1 detached house, 2 bungalow, 3 cottage, 4 caravan, 5 apartment block / block of flats, 6 motor home, 7 semi-detached house, 8 terraced house

3a   **House swapping**   5 mins

    Tip: Reading skills (3) We can help students to learn to read for gist (overall meaning) by setting a very general question for them to answer after their first reading of a text.

- ↓ Say: *Read the ad on page 21 and decide which information is correct.*
  Board: It's an advert for cheap / free holiday accommodation. (free)
- Follow coursebook instructions.
  You stay in someone else's private house and they stay in yours.

3b Text   **Reading**   5 mins
- Before students read the main part of the text, remind them that it isn't necessary to understand every single word. Allow time for them to read the text to themselves.
- Ask the gist question.
  They thought the two brothers were stealing from their neighbour's house.

4a   **What can you remember?**   5 mins
- Follow coursebook instructions.

4b   **Talk about it**   5 mins
- Follow coursebook instructions.

5a   **Focus on ...** *for / ago*   5 mins
- Read out the three sentences in the *Focus on* box and the explanation underneath.
- Ask which sentences are about the past. (sentences 1 + 3)

Extra

for / ago 10 mins	
• Board: I had my very first English lesson ...	I learnt English at school ...
I came to this school ...	I've been in this school ...
I moved to this town ...	I've lived in this town ...
I started my present job ...	I've worked for my present company ...
• Students complete four sentences which are relevant to them using *for* or *ago* and read them to the class.	

5b   **Now you: Your home**   5+ mins
- ↓ Go through the questions and decide which answers need *for* and which need *ago*.
- Board: *   Choose three questions to ask.
        **   As in the coursebook.
        ***   Add one more question of your own.

    1 for, 2 for, 3 ago, 4 ago, 5 ago, 6 for

If short of time
- Do *Exercise 6a* as a class activity.
- In *Exercise 6b*, ask a few individuals to describe their home to the class.
- Do *Exercise 7* for homework (and then display their work in the next lesson).

6a   **Vocabulary building: Compound adjectives**   5 mins
    ! Tell the class that these words usually have hyphens in them but, slowly, hyphens are becoming old-fashioned so they may see these words without hyphens.
    ! English speakers usually say how many bedrooms their home has, not how many square metres.

    1 the forty-pound registration fee, 2 a 300-year-old cottage, 3 their two-bedroom flat, 4 their two-week stay 5 a two-day city break, 6 a four-star hotel, 7 a ten-hour flight, 8 a three-month holiday, 9 a fifty-mile journey, 10 a fifteen-storey building

6b Describing your home 10 mins
1e), 2f), 3h), 4g), 5b), 6d), 7a), 8c)

7 Writing 10 mins
- Suggest that students write in pencil so that they can correct mistakes before their work is displayed.

8 What do you think? 5 mins
- Class or group discussion prompted by the saying.
- ↓ If necessary, prompt: *Where do you think of as home? Why?*

Unit 1 Now I can

Contents Review of vocabulary, functions and structures in Unit 1

Lesson notes

www You can download and copy a **Project sheet** to be used for the writing activities in *Now I can*: www.klett-langenscheidt.de/networknow/activities (Unit 1: Now I can)

Now I can: ... 5 mins
- Ask students to look at *Now I can: ...* at the top of p. 24. Remind them that the symbols refer to different skills or vocabulary items they learnt in Unit 1 and were listed in the unit aims on p. 9.

Starter Talking about people's living arrangements/relationships; Describing someone's personality 5+ mins

Look back
Possible answers: **Lena: divorced, Swedish, 3 children, re-married, is patient, cheerful, creative and untidy. Karl: divorced, re-married, new baby, good father, reliable, generous, patient, but very tidy and a control freak. Shaun: lives with his partner and 3 children, has a crocodile zoo, kept crocodiles in his garden.**

Now look forward
- Ask if anyone has been to an English-speaking country and ask for a few details.

Part 1 Talking about people's living arrangements; Describing someone's personality

1a Language exchange 5+ mins
- Get one student to note down the advantages on the board and one to note down the disadvantages.
- Ask for ideas how to get over the disadvantages.

1b Come and stay with me! 10 mins
! If you have downloaded and copied the Project sheet, you can use it for this exercise, *Exercise 3b* and 4.

Part 2 Describing someone's personality; Talking about relationships

2a A good relationship? 5 mins
- Read out the instructions and play ▶ 1/17.

They got on really well. No, but Ruth emails her sometimes.

(F = friend, R = Ruth) F: Ruth, you've done a language exchange, haven't you? How did you get on with your French exchange partner? R: Oh, great. Really well. Sylvie, she was called. Actually, we're still friends now, six months later. F: Oh, that's nice. R: Yes, it is. I wouldn't say we're best friends, or really close, but I email her sometimes and tell	her what I'm doing and it's always nice to hear from her. I'm quite fond of her and I'd be happy to see her again. F: You were lucky to find someone you got on with. R: Well, we don't have the same sort of personality, but that didn't matter. It was good for me to be with someone who showed me a different lifestyle.

2b **What were they like?** 10 mins

🔊 1/18

- ↓ Make A and B groups. A students underline the words for Sylvie; B students circle the words for Pascal.

🔑 Sylvie: <u>confident</u>, <u>generous</u>, <u>spontaneous</u>; Pascal: (patient), (shy)

(F = friend, R = Ruth)

F: So, you say that this Sylvie is quite different from you. What's she like? What do you like about her?

R: The main thing I like about Sylvie is that she's full of energy and ideas. One morning we were having breakfast and she suddenly said, "Let's go to the mountains for the day," so we did. Just like that.

F: Yes, that's quite different from you!

R: You're right. I'm the sort of person who likes to organise things weeks in advance, so it was good for me to be a bit freer. Last month she decided to look for a new job and she gave up her old job before she found a new one. She said, "I know I can get a better job. I'm good at what I do and someone will want me." She never thinks, "Oh, I might not be able to do this." She just does things and of course everything works out fine. I'd like to be more like her.

F: Me, too!

R: And another thing about Sylvie. When she found that I was between jobs during the exchange, and didn't have so much money, she paid for a lot of things for me – meals, train tickets, all sorts of things. I said, "No, you can't do this, I can't pay you back," but she always said, "Oh, don't worry, you're my guest."

F: Oh, that was nice of her.

R: Yes, it was. And she has a lovely boyfriend. He's quite different from Sylvie. Pascal, he's called. He doesn't like meeting new people so much. I didn't meet him for the first three or four days of my stay. When you get to know him, just you and him together, he's very clever and funny, but in a big group of people, he's quite quiet. Yes, more like me than like Sylvie, really.

F: And did you speak a lot of French?

R: Yes, I did. Before I went to France, I was a bit worried because my French wasn't very good. Sylvie and Pascal's English was much better than my French – much, much better! I spoke so slowly at first and really had to search for the right word all the time, but they were really good with me. Sylvie always tried to guess what I wanted to say – "Do you mean this, or do you mean that?" – which was helpful. But Pascal had a different tactic. He listened really carefully and tried really hard to understand and he never looked bored or annoyed. He and I got on very well. Really, very well.

F: Oh?!

Part 3 **Describing someone's personality; Talking about relationships; Describing a visit**

3a **This is my best friend** 10 mins
- Demonstrate the activity with a photo of yours – this will act as a pattern for students to follow.
- Students work with a partner and then report their ideas back to the class.

If short of time
- Do *Exercise 3b* as a class activity.

3b **We had a guided tour** 10 mins
- You can use the Project sheet for this exercise.

Part 4 **Talking about accommodation**

I'd like to stay longer 10 mins
- You can use the Project sheet for this exercise.
- **!** pcm = per calendar month

5 **Now you choose** 10 mins
- Remind students about the star system and tell them they can choose one of the tasks.
- Students work with a partner. (It doesn't matter if they've chosen the same or different tasks.)

And finally 5 mins • Look back at the *In this unit, you will learn to: …* (p. 9) to show your students how much they have learnt in this unit and say how well they've done.
- Show them the homework pages for this lesson – the *Test yourself* pages (pp. 26/27).
- If you don't plan to use the extra pages (*English worldwide, English at work* and *Story*) in the lesson, students can enjoy these pages at home.

Unit 2 Step 1 My light bulb moment

Contents

Text topic A magazine article about having good ideas
Functions Giving detailed accounts of experiences; Presenting information in an interesting way
Vocabulary Creative activities
Grammar **You already know:** Past progressive / past simple
And now: *when / while*

Lesson notes

www **Extra activity:** www.klett-langenscheidt.de/networknow/activities (Unit 2: Step 1)

Starter 5 mins • Ask individual students the *Starter* questions.
Possible answers: **to keep the door open, to throw through a jeweller's window, …**

1a **Vocabulary: Creative activities** 5 mins
Beethoven: composed music, Versace: designed clothes, Picasso: painted pictures, Shakespeare: wrote plays, Edison: invented the light bulb
• ↑ After students have made sentences about the five people, ask volunteers to think of other creative people and make sentences about them.

1b **A man of ideas** 10 mins
Tip: Setting up listenings (2) Your students might feel nervous about listening exercises because they don't understand every word and they're worried they'll 'miss' something. For this reason, it's a good idea to play the track – or parts of the track – more than once, and give students support with the task.
• ↓ Board: 1 He invented the l_____ b_____, the p_____, the m_____ p_____ c_____, a b_____ for an electric car.
Play ▶ 1/26 up to: … *an electric car* and have volunteers supply the answers.
Board: 2 He went to school for _____. He trained as a _____.
Play ▶ 1/26 from the beginning up to: … *as a telegraph operator*. Have volunteers supply the answers.
Board: 3 Bad luck: experiment – burnt – job / Good luck: repair – telegraph office – head
Play ▶ 1/26 from the beginning to the end and have volunteers supply the answers.
• Play ▶ 1/26.
Possible answers: **1 Edison invented the light bulb. / He discovered how we could use and generate electrical power. / He invented the phonograph / the motion picture camera / and he made a battery for an electric car. 2 Edison only had three months of school education. He trained as a telegraph operator. 3 Bad luck: When Edison was doing an experiment with a battery, he burnt his boss's desk and lost his job. Good luck: Edison was able to repair the machine in a telegraph office and was given a job as the head of the whole office.**

> Lecturer:
> Thomas Alva Edison was an American inventor who lived through one of the greatest periods of discovery and invention in history and he himself was responsible for much of it.
> So, what did Edison invent? Well, we know him as the man who invented the light bulb. But he didn't only invent the light bulb. For example – did you know? – he was one of the first people to discover how we could generate and use electrical power. He invented the phonograph, which was a machine that could record and play sound. He also invented the motion picture camera, to make movies. And maybe you don't know this, but he made a battery for an electric car.
> So, how did a poor boy, born in Ohio, who only had three months of school education in his life become one of our greatest inventors, with over one thousand US patents to his name?
> Now, this is really interesting. When he was in his teens, he saved a little boy's life. The boy's father was so grateful that he trained the young Edison as a telegraph operator.
> Now, have you ever heard of Western Union, the big finance and communications company? Well, Edison got his first job as a telegraph operator for Western Union.

He asked to work at night, so he could have more time during the day for reading and inventing. One day at work, he was doing an experiment with a battery when he had an accident and, unfortunately, he burnt his boss's desk. His boss wasn't pleased and so Edison lost his job. He moved to New York City with nothing, without a cent.

He was looking for a job in New York when he had a bit of good luck. I'll tell you what happened. He was visiting a telegraph office when the machine broke. Edison was able to repair it and he was given a job – not just as a telegraph operator, but as the head of the whole office, with a salary of 300 dollars a month.

But Edison was never very interested in money. He once said, "My main purpose in life is to make enough money to create ever more inventions."

While he was working in New York, Edison was able to spend more time working on his experiments and his inventions.

2a   **Look again**   5 mins
The first half of each sentence gives us the background to the event.
The second half of each sentence tells us what happened.

2b   **Grammar: You already know – Past progressive / past simple**   5– mins
• Focus attention on the Grammar box and ask: *Which verb is in the past progressive tense?* (was looking) *Which verb is in the past simple tense?* (had)
! For more explanations and practice, you can look at the Language study on page 35.

2c   **Now you: Key moments in your life**   10 mins
• Demonstrate the activity by telling the class about something in your life.

Text   **My light bulb moment**   5+ mins
Tip: Reading skills (4) Give the students time to read the texts to themselves. It isn't a good idea to have them read it aloud because then they focus on pronunciation and can't concentrate on the meaning. If they want to hear the text, remind them that they can listen to the text when the do *Exercise 1* on the *Selfstudy* page (p. 36).

3   **Who is it?**   5+ mins
1 Shona Finlay, Mimi Kellard; 2 Peter Moody, Barbara Swanney; 3 Barbara Swanney, Shona Finlay; 4 Barbara Swanney; 5 Barbara Swanney, Shona Finlay; 6 Peter Moody, Mimi Kellard

4a   **Grammar: And now –** *when / while*   5 mins
• Focus attention on the Grammar box and have students repeat the sentences.
! For more explanations and practice, you can look at the Language study on page 35.

Extra

When / while 10 mins		
• Board:		

	he was sleeping,	someone kicked a ball through the window.
	she was having a shower,	the doorbell rang.
While	they were doing their homework,	my aunt arrived.
	I was phoning my sister,	the baby woke up.
	we were watching TV,	the dog started to bark.

• Ask individuals to combine words from each column to make sentences, beginning with *While … .*
• Then rub out the word *While* and write *when* in the middle column and have individuals make sentences with *when* in the middle.

4b   **What were they doing?**   10 mins
1 Peter was cooking when he burnt his finger. Peter burnt his finger when / while he was cooking. 2 Barbara was working in her office when one of her client's phoned with a problem. One of Barbara's clients phoned with a problem when / while she was working in her office. 3 Shona's pupils were sharing a lesson with pupils in India when the Internet connection crashed. The Internet connection crashed when / while Shona's pupils were sharing a lesson with pupils in India. 4 Mimi was having lunch at the day centre when she met Barry, a new volunteer. Mimi met Barry, a new volunteer, when / while she was having lunch at the day centre.

5a   **How to present information in an interesting way**   5 mins
- Play ▶ 1/27.

   ✓ **Did you know?; Maybe you don't know this, but …; Now, this is really interesting.; Have you ever heard of …?; I'll tell you what happened.**

   | Audio script: see track 1/26 above. |

If short of time   • Suggest that for *Exercise 5b*, they phone a classmate the following day and present their talk.

5b   **Now you choose: A short talk**   10+ mins
- Students choose which task they'd like to do and then present their talk to a partner – they don't need to have chosen the same task.

6   **What do you think?**   5+ mins
- Students work in groups of 3 or 4 and give their opinions on the topics.

Unit 2 Step 2 Under attack!

Contents

Text topic   An online article about guerrilla knitting
Functions   Giving an opinion; Expressing feelings in an email
Vocabulary   Emotional reactions
Grammar   Past perfect

Lesson notes

www   **Extra activity:** www.klett-langenscheidt.de/networknow/activities (Unit 2: Step 2)

Starter   5 mins   • Ask individual students the *Starter* questions.
   Possible answers: **socks, scarves, gloves, pullovers, baby clothes**

Text   **Under attack!**   5 mins
- Give students time to read the article to themselves and then ask: *Where does the story take place?* (in Canada) *Which things were 'decorated'?* (trees, parking meters, the park, a bicycle, statues, a mail box)

1   **What's your reaction?**   5+ mins
- The statements can be discussed in class or in groups.

2a   **Grammar: Past perfect**   5– mins
- Read out the first sentence from the Grammar box and have students repeat it in chorus.
- Ask: *Did the guerrillas decorate the town before the people woke up or after?* (before)
   ! For more explanations and practice, you can look at the Language study on page 40.

2b   **What can you remember?**   10 mins
- ↓ Give prompts. Board: jackets – trees, flowers – park, bicycle – library, hats – statues
   Possible answers: **Someone … had decorated Pinetown during the night – with wool. … had covered the town with knitted creations. … had put woollen jackets on trees and parking meters. … had planted knitted flowers in the park. … had parked a knitted bicycle outside the library. … had put knitted hats and scarves onto the statues in the museum gardens. … had knitted a cover for a mail box.**
- Write the sentence on the board: They had put jackets on trees.
- Tell students that *had put* is the past perfect tense. It's made with *had* + the third form of the verb (*give, gave, **given***). It's used when we're talking about a situation in the past and we want to say that something had happened before that.

Extra

> *Past perfect*   10 mins
> - Say: *We use the 'past simple' to talk about events in a chronological order.*
> - Board: make breakfast – wake up – get up – have a shower – clean my teeth – go to work – listen to the news – have a cup of coffee – eat breakfast
> - Ask the class to write a sentence about three things they did this morning: *This morning, I …*
> - Ask individuals to read out their sentences, e.g. *This morning, I got up, I had a shower and then I ate breakfast.*
> - Then ask them to write this sentence and complete it with a time: *My alarm clock had rung at …*
> - Ask: *Which tense is 'had rung'?* (past perfect) *Did this happen before or after the other events?* (before)
> - Ask students to complete this text, writing the verbs in the correct tenses.
>   Board: Last week, I (meet) _____ an old friend. We (have) _____ lunch together and (talk) _____ about our student days. We (study) _____ together at Bristol University. At two o'clock, we (say) _____ goodbye and we (go) _____ back to work.

   met, had, talked, had studied, said, went

2c   **What had happened?**   5+ mins

Possible answers: **1** … had a difficult test. / … been on a school trip. / … had a lot of different subjects. / … learnt a lot of new things. **2** … he'd found his lost cat. / … he'd had a lot of fun playing football with his friends. / … he'd met his new girlfriend. **3** … he/she had won the lottery. / … he/she had had an accident.

2d   **Now you: Your experiences**   10– mins
- After the pairwork, ask volunteers to tell the class their experience. Then ask: *And how did you feel about it?*

3a   **Vocabulary: Emotional reactions**   10+ mins

- Play ▶ 1/34 so students can listen and repeat before deciding whether the words are positive or negative.

Positive reactions: **delighted, grateful, pleased, proud**; Negative reactions: **disappointed, shocked, upset**; Both, positive and negative reactions: **amazed, surprised**
- Demonstrate the next task by making a sentence with one of the words, e.g. *I was amazed because I had passed my driving test!*
- Students work in pairs and make sentences with the words.
- Board: *   I was … because my best friend had …
            **   As in the coursebook.
            ***   I was … because … and so I …

3b   **What's their reaction?**   5+ mins

1/35–36

Speaker 1: negative reaction, Speaker 2: mixed reaction, Speaker 3: positive reaction;
I think …: speaker 3; In my opinion, …: speaker 1; To be honest, …: speaker 2; I find it …: speaker 2

> (RI = radio interviewer, S1 = speaker 1, S2 = speaker 2, S3 = speaker 3)
> **1**
> RI: Excuse me, sir. What do you think about the yarnbombing attack on our town?
> S1:   Oh, you mean that knitting thing?
> RI: That's right. What's your opinion?
> S1:   Oh, I'm not very pleased about it. Not very pleased at all. Someone will have to clear it up – it's a waste of time and money!
> RI: You don't think it's a just bit of fun?
> S1:   I don't understand it. In my opinion, these people should have to clear it up themselves.
> **2**
> RI: Excuse me. What do you think about the yarnbombing attack?
> S2:   The what?
> RI: The guerrilla knitting. Did you see it in the news?
> S2:   Oh, yeah. I was surprised by people's reactions.
> RI: How do you mean, 'surprised'?
> S2:   I saw a lot of people were upset about it, but I don't get that.

RI: So, what's your reaction?

S2: Me? I don't mind it. Well, to be honest, I don't really understand it. I find it all a bit silly, all these silly knitted things in the streets. It's fun for kids but not really something for adults. But it doesn't hurt anyone, so – why not?

3

RI: Excuse me. Can I ask you – what's your reaction to the yarnbombing attack?

S3: I think it's amazing.

RI: So you like it, then?

S3: Yeah, sure. It's fun.

RI: What do you like about it?

S3: The town is so full of color and full of surprises. You never know what you're going to see next! Did you see the knitted bike? It's really cute.

RI: Do you think it's good for the image of the town?

S3: Yeah, why not? I think it looks good and I'm proud of our town.

4a **How to give an opinion** 5– mins
- Read out the phrases and have the class repeat them in chorus.

4b **Now you: What's your opinion?** 5+ mins

Tip: Discussion When students are working in pairs or groups, encourage discussion by prompting with follow-up questions, e.g. *Why do you think that? / Do you agree?*

- Monitor the activity and encourage students to give reasons for their opinions.

If short of time
- Do *Exercise 5a* as a class activity.
- *Exercise 5b:* Suggest they write the email on their home computers and send it to a classmate.

5a **An email** 5 mins
- Ask students how they can begin an email to a friend. (Dear …, Hi …, Hello …)
- Ask students how they can end an email to a friend. (Love from …, Best wishes …, Yours …)

5b **Dear …** 5 mins
- Read out the instructions and the headline and ask what *freak weather* could be. (storm, flood, tornado, tsunami)

Possible answer:

Re: Freak weather

Hi …

I was very sorry to read about your town in our newspaper here in the UK. What a shocking story!
You must feel very upset to see your town in the international news.
What about you? Has the weather damaged your house as well?
We must speak soon. Let me know when you have time and I'll call you.

Love from
…

6 **What do you think?** 5+ mins

Info In 2009, Paris's Pompidou Centre devoted an entire exhibition to the art of nothing.
- In class, students give their opinions on the picture.
- Encourage discussion by asking follow-up questions: *What was the last exhibition you saw? What public works of art are there in your town? What pictures do you have in your home?*

Unit 2 Step 3 Upcycling

Contents

Text topic   Washing instructions on a clothes label
Functions   Talking about clothes and accessories
Vocabulary Clothes and accessories; Adjectives ending in -able / -ful / -y; British and American English
Grammar   Focus on: *during / while*
Reading   How 'trashionable' are you?

Lesson notes

www   **Extra activity:** www.klett-langenscheidt.de/networknow/activities (Unit 2: Step 3)

Info   Conserve India really exists so encourage your students to visit Conserve India's website.

Starter   5 mins • Ask individual students the *Starter* questions and get them to give their reasons.

1   **Close-up: Clothes labels**   5 mins

                 Tip: Realia (2) Using realia when you're teaching can make your lessons more authentic. Students see 'real-life' things which they can expect to find in English-speaking countries. Remember when using realia that learners will probably be faced with some unknown vocabulary – just as they would be in a real-life situation – and that it isn't necessary for them to understand every individual word.

                 ✓ 1, 6

2a   **Clothes and accessories**   10 mins
                 • Point out that the word *purse* in British English is where you keep your money; the word purse in American English is what the British call a *handbag*. Tell them that they'll be looking at more BE and AE differences later in the lesson.
                 • ↓ Brainstorm *clothes* by playing *I packed my case*: A: *I packed a pair of jeans.* B: *I packed a pair of jeans and a pullover.* C: *I packed a pair of jeans, a pullover and …*
                 • Ask two volunteers to stand back-to-back in front of the class and describe what the partner is wearing.

2b   **Now you: Your clothes**   5+ mins
                 • Remind the class to use the different tenses *(wore, would wear, going to wear)*.

3   **Vocabulary building: Adjectives ending in -able / -ful / -y**   5+ mins
                 • As students call out the answers, write them on the board and encourage students to write them down, too.
                 beautiful, careful, cleanable, colourful, dirty, healthy, recyclable, reusable, trendy
                 After the football match, my T-shirt was really dirty.

4a   **Upcycling**   5 mins
                 • Students read the first paragraph only and answer the question.
                 Upcycling is when you make fashion from trash. This fashion is called 'trashion'. Waste is kept in its original form and colour and reused to make completely different products with a higher value than the original product.

4b Text   **Reading**   10 mins

                 Tip: Reading skills (5) Get students to underline the relevant information in the text – this will make it easier for them to answer the questions.

                 1 Converse India makes its products from plastic bags, car tires and seatbelts, textiles like cotton, denim and old saris.
                 2 It uses the money it makes to finance education and health projects for slum families, including their own employees.

5 **What can you remember?**   10+ mins
- ↓ First let students work in pairs and underline the relevant information in the text. Then compare answers in class.
  Possible answers:
  – India produces millions of tonnes of waste every year. It would be impossible to recycle so much waste. So Anita and Shalabh Ahuja came up with the idea of upcycling.
  – Converse employs about 1,000 local people from the slums. They usually have no education or skills. The company trains them to collect and process plastic and other waste and make the products. The people who collect the waste are called 'rag pickers'. Converse pays them for the amount of waste they bring in. They earn about three times more than they would from other jobs.
  – Plastic waste is washed, dried and pressed into a material called 'Handmade Recycled Plastic'. This is used to create beautiful, colorful accessories.
  – Anita and her team design the products.
  – They sell most of their products abroad, especially in the USA, Europe, Israel, Japan and Australia. The advantage is that they can make more money there.

6a **Focus on ...** *during / while*   5– mins
- Read out the example sentences and the explanation in the *Focus on ...* box.

Extra

during / while   10 mins
- Call out prompts and ask two students to complete the sentences – one student with *while* + activity and one student with something that happened, like this:
Prompt: *During the night ...*
Student 1:   *During the night, while I was sleeping ...*
Student 2:   *During the night, while I was sleeping, someone broke into my house.*
(Prompts: *During my holiday ... / During the party ... / During the lesson ... / During the flight ... / During the concert ... / During breakfast ... / During the meeting ... / During the film ...)*

6b **Working at Conserve India**   5+ mins
- Let students work in pairs to decide on the answers before asking volunteers to read out the sentences to the class.
  (1) During | ~~While~~ (2) ~~during~~ | while (3) during | ~~while~~ (4) ~~During~~ | While (5) ~~during~~ | while (6) during | ~~while~~

If short of time
- In *Exercise 7a*, instead of searching for the words in the text, write the list of American words on the board (see page 142 in the coursebook) and ask the class to say what the British English word or spelling is.

7a **British and American English**   10 mins
! The key is on page 142 of the coursebook.

7b *Jewellery* or *jewelry*?   5+ mins
BE: swimming costume = AE: bathing suit, BE: handbag = AE: purse, BE: trousers = AE: pants, BE: knickers = AE: panties, BE: jewellery = AE: jewelry, BE: jumper/pullover = AE: sweater, BE: pyjamas = AE: pajamas, BE: (under)pants = AE: shorts, BE: purse = AE: money-purse, BE: vest = AE: undershirt, BE: tights = AE: pantyhose, BE: trainers = AE: sneakers

8 **What do you think?**   5+ mins
- Class discussion prompted by the quotation. If necessary, ask follow-up questions, e.g. *What's the worst thing you (or your children) have worn?*

Unit 2 Now I can

| **Contents** | Review of vocabulary, functions and structures in Unit 2 |

Lesson notes

| www | You can download and copy a **Project sheet** to be used for the writing activities in *Now I can*: www.klett-langenscheidt.de/networknow/activities (Unit 2: Now I can) |

| Now I can: ... | 5 mins | • Ask students to look at *Now I can: ...* at the top of p. 46. Remind them that the symbols refer to different skills or vocabulary items they learnt in Unit 2 and were listed in the unit aims on p. 31. |

| Starter | **Giving detailed accounts of experiences; Expressing feelings and reactions; Talking about clothes and accessories** 5+ mins |

| Look back 🔑 | Possible answers: **Bulb – The great American Thomas Edison invented the light bulb and had over one thousand patents. Knitted bicycle – A local knitting group covered a Canadian town with knitted creations, like knitted flowers. Guerilla knitting has become a trend. Bag –a product of Converse India, an upcycling company that makes fashion from trash.** |

| Now look forward | • Ask what is meant here by *style*. (clothes, hairstyle, appearance) |

| Part 1 | **Giving personal opinions; Talking about clothes and accessories** |

| 1a | **What's your style?** 10 mins
! If you have downloaded and copied the Project sheet, you can use it for this exercise, *Exercise 1b, 2c, 2d* and *3*.
 • ↓ Board: Do you often wear ...? Where did you get ...? Have you ever worn ...? What's your favourite ...? |

| 1b | **What's your opinion?** 10 mins
• You can use the Project sheet for this exercise.
• Monitor the activity and prompt more reluctant students with: *What do you think about (piercings)?* |

| Part 2 | **Giving detailed accounts of experiences; Giving personal opinions; Expressing feelings and reactions; Talking about clothes and accessories** |

| 2a | **What do you look like?!** 5 mins
• ↓ Brainstorm positive and negative adjectives by replacing the underlined words.
   Board: She looks <u>awful</u>.   She looks <u>amazing</u>.
         (terrible, horrible, ...)   (fantastic, great, ...) |

| 2b 🔊 1/43–44 🔑 | **Home from university** 10+ mins
• Read out the instructions and play ▶ 1/43.

1 lip, 2 family event
Possible answers: **Katy's father doesn't like her piercing and can't understand why his daughter has decided to have one. Chris's father is surprised about his son's new clothes and how good he looks.** |

(F1 = father 1, F2 = father 2)	F1: Oh, I see, yes, that's not so nice.
F1: Your Katy must be home from university now, for the summer.	F2: No, but she's so pleased with it. Of course she's an adult now and I'm just her old-fashioned dad, so I can't say anything, but –
F2: Yes, she is. She came home on Saturday ... with a piercing. I couldn't believe it.	oh, why didn't she stop and think before she did it? She's a clever girl, but to be honest, I
F1: Don't you like it?	think she's made a silly mistake. You do
F2: No, I don't. It's a big piece of metal and it's there, where everyone can see it.	something like that, and you have a hole in your face for ever.

F1: Do you know why she got it? Had she wanted one for a long time?

F2: No, I don't think so. She says it was totally spontaneous. You see, she was really happy because she'd received her exam results that morning and she'd passed all her exams. In fact, she was top of the class in three of her subjects. She was delighted. So, anyway, she was walking through the town centre when she saw a tattoo and piercing salon and she says it was a totally spontaneous idea. She decided to go into the salon and get a piercing to celebrate her success.

F1: Oh, is that how they celebrate these days? In our day, we went to the pub and had a few beers.

F2: I don't know how she can drink, or eat, or do *anything*, with that big piece of metal in her lip. Oh, it looks awful! And I can feel it when she kisses me. My beautiful girl, with a piercing. I don't understand it. But, anyway, that's enough about Katy – your Chris must be home from university, too.

F1: Yes, he is. He's been home since Friday. Well, he already had a piercing and a tattoo before he went to university, so I know how you feel! But he's surprised us with a new look, too.

F2: Really?

F1: Yes, he came home for the summer in his usual style – you know, old jeans, T-shirt, trainers, a bit of a beard.

F2: Oh yes.

F1: And the next morning, he came downstairs and he was a totally new man. He looked so different.

F2: In what way?

F1: Well, he'd washed his hair, he'd shaved and he was wearing a very smart suit – and a tie!

F2: A suit and tie? Your Chris?

F1: Yes, an expensive one, with a very stylish shirt. I'd never seen him like that before. And I must say he looked really good.

F2: And why the change? Was it a special occasion?

F1: Yes, his new girlfriend had invited him to her sister's wedding and he didn't want to disappoint her.

F2: Well, good for him.

2c **Tell the story** 10 mins
- You can use the Project sheet for this exercise.

  Katy was really happy because she had received her exam results. She was walking through the town centre when she saw a tattoo and piercing salon. It was a totally spontaneous idea. She decided to go into the salon and get a piercing to celebrate her success. Chris came downstairs and looked so different. He had washed his hair, he had shaved and was wearing a very smart suit and a tie. His new girlfriend had invited him to her sister's wedding and he didn't want to disappoint her.

2d **I was really surprised** 5+ mins
- You can use the Project sheet for this exercise.
- Demonstrate the activity by telling the class about someone in your family – this will act as a pattern for them to follow.

If short of time
- Do *Exercise 3* as a class activity, with students from each group volunteering information.

Part 3 **Presenting information in an interesting way**

Tattoo facts 10+ mins
- You can use the Project sheet for this exercise.
- Before doing the pairwork activity, divide the class into A and B groups and let them read and discuss their texts in the group.
- Students discuss the information and then report back to the group.

4 **Now you choose** 10 mins
- Remind students about the star system and tell them they can choose one of the tasks.
- Students find a partner who wants to do the same task and they work together.

And finally 5 mins • Look back at the *In this unit, you will learn to:* ... (p. 31) to show your students how much they have learnt in this unit and say how well they've done.
- Remind students about the homework pages for this lesson – the *Test yourself* pages (pp. 48/49).
- If you don't plan to use the extra pages (*English worldwide* and *English at work*) in the lesson, students can enjoy these pages at home.

Unit 3 Step 1 Let's grow!

Contents

Text topic An advert for the organisation 'lendwithcare.org'
Functions Talking about plans, intentions and decisions; Describing a business
Vocabulary Business sectors
Grammar **You already know:** *going to, planning to, intend to* for plans and intentions
And now: *will* for spontaneous decisions

Lesson notes

www **Extra activity:** www.klett-langenscheidt.de/networknow/activities (Unit 3: Step 1)

Info Students can learn more about the organisation by typing *lendwithcare.org* into their search engine.

Starter *5– mins* • Ask individual students the *Starter* questions.
Possible answer:
You borrow money from your bank / Your bank lends you money and when you pay it back you have to pay interest – a per cent of what you borrowed.

1a **Change a life with a loan** 5+ mins
• Students read the advert to themselves and do the task.
• Answers are then compared in class.
1 a charity, 2 lend, 3 minimum, 4 doesn't mention

1b **What's the motivation?** 5+ mins
The lender wants to help; the borrower wants to start a business and be independent.

1c Text **What are they going to do?** 10 mins
• ↓ Divide the class into A and B groups. Group A reads and answers questions about Nisveta; Group B reads and answers questions about Emmanuel.
1 Nisveta, Emmanuel, 2 Nisveta, 3 Emmanuel, 4 Nisveta, 5 neither, 6 Emmanuel

2a **Look again** 5 mins
• Ask students to underline the phrases used to talk about plans.
They use *going to ...*, *planning to ...* and *intend to ...* .

2b **Grammar: You already know – Expressing plans and intentions** 5+ mins
NB *Intend* is normally used in the simple form, not the progressive form.
• Focus attention on the Grammar box and read out the sentences. Then ask volunteers to rephrase the sentences, using one of the other two ways of expressing plans. (Nisveta **is planning to / intends to** develop ... Emmanuel **is going to / intends to** offer ... Emmanuel **is going to / is planning to** pay back ...)
! For more explanations and practice, you can look at the Language study on page 57.

2c **Now you: What are you planning to do?** 5+ mins
• Demonstrate the activity by telling the class some of your plans – use the three forms: *going to, intend to* and *planning to*, e.g. *My mother-in-law is planning to visit us next week so I'm going to clean the house at the weekend. I intend to have everything perfect!*

3 **I'm going to make a loan** 5+ mins
• Read out the first part of the task and then play ▶ 2/2.
2/2–3 • Play ▶ 2/3 and ask students to tick the phrases they hear.
The loan is already complete.
1 I'll choose another one.
2 I'll give it to the mechanic.

(M = man, W = woman)
M: This is such a good idea, this Lend with care website. It's great. In fact, I've decided that I'm going to to make a loan.
W: That's good.
M: Yes, I'm going to lend £15 to this woman here. She's a farmer in Bosnia. So I just need to click here and ... oh!
W: What's the matter?
M: It says 'This loan is now complete'. Ah, so she has the full amount of money.
W: Oh, so you can't lend to her.
M: No, I can't. But it doesn't matter. I'll choose another one. er ... This one looks good. He's a mechanic. And his loan isn't complete yet. That's good. So, yes, I'll give it to the mechanic. I'll just click here and enter my payment details and it's done.

4a **Grammar: And now – *will* for spontaneous decisions**   5– mins
• Read out the sentence in the Grammar box.
• Ask how to make a negative sentence:
  Board: I_____ lend it to the farmer. (won't)
! For more explanations and practice, you can look at the Language study on page 57.

Extra

> **Spontaneous decisions**   5+ mins
> • Read out the prompts so that students can use *will* to express a spontaneous decision:
>   It's very warm in this room. (I'll open the window.)
>   There's someone at the door. (I'll open it.)
>   My phone is ringing and I'm washing my hair. (I'll answer it.)
>   My homework's really difficult. (I'll help you.)
>   I can't read that notice. (I'll read it for you.)

If short of time
• Do the first part of *Exercise 4b* as a class activity.

Tip: Photos Exploit the photos that are in the coursebook. For example, in *Exercise 4b*, get students to tell you where the photos were taken (restaurant, railway station, office) and to speculate about the situation, e.g. It's the couple's 50th wedding anniversary and they're at their favourite Italian restaurant. Encourage the use of the present progressive when describing a photo. (The waiter **is writing** down their order.)

4b **OK then, I'll ...**   10– mins

2/4–5
• Have students talk about the photos before you play ▶ 2/4.
• Play ▶ 2/5 and ask students to check their answers to the first part of the task.
  Possible answers: **1 ... have the vegetable soup / egg salad / pizza margherita. 2 ... take the slow train / fast train, but not first class. 3 ... call again.**

> (The underlined sentences are not recorded in Track 4.)
> **1** (C = customer, W = waiter)
> C: I'm looking for something vegetarian.
> W: How about the vegetable soup? Or there's pizza margherita. And a lot of our salads are vegetarian. There's egg salad, or cheese, ...
> C: OK then, I'll have the pizza margherita, please.
>
> **2** (P = passenger, E = ticket office employee)
> P: I'd like a day return to Bristol, please.
> E: OK. There's a fast train or a slow train. The difference in time is about an hour and the difference in price is about £30. And, if you're interested, on the fast train you can pay extra to upgrade to first class.
> P: Er ... I think I'll take the fast train. But not first class.
>
> **3** (C = caller, PA = personal assistant)
> C: Hello. Could I speak to the head of planning, please?
> PA: Oh I'm sorry. He's out on a site visit this morning, until about 12. I can take a message if you like.
> C: Oh, no, it's fine. I'll call again this afternoon. It isn't urgent.

5a Vocabulary: Business sectors   5+ mins
• Play ▶ 2/6. Students listen and repeat the vocabulary before using the words in sentences.

Possible answers: **building:** Bilfinger Berger Hochbau, Hochtief AG; **fashion:** Versace, Esprit; **financial services:** Deutsche Bank; **food and drink:** Nestlé; **pharmaceutical:** Merck, La Roche, Ratiopharm; **publishing:** Gruner und Jahr, Bertelsmann; **retail:** Aldi, Galeria Kaufhof; **sport and leisure:** Adidas, Nike, Reebok; **technology:** Samsung, Siemens, Apple, Microsoft; **tourism:** Neckermann, Tui, Thomas Cook

5b How to describe a business   5+ mins
• Say: Let's talk about Aldi. Ask volunteers to read out each phrase and make it apply to Aldi. (Aldi is in the retail sector. It sells food. It's customers are from all social classes. It has lots of shops in lots of countries. It has a lot of hard-working employees. It's very successful. It was started by the Albrecht brothers.)

5c Now you: Who do you work for?   10– mins
• Follow coursebook instructions.

6 What do you think?   5+ mins
• Students work in groups of 3 or 4 and give their opinions by completing the sentences.

Unit 3 Step 2 Protest!

Contents

Text topic A letter of complaint
Functions Saying how and why people protest; Expressing preference
Vocabulary Reasons to protest
Grammar **You already know:** First conditional
And now: *unless*

Lesson notes

www **Extra activity:** www.klett-langenscheidt.de/networknow/activities (Unit 3: Step 2)

Starter 5 mins • Ask individual students the *Starter* question.

Info **Leipzig:** Peaceful demonstrations by East German citizens, demanding to travel freely and to be able to elect a democratic government, took place on Monday evenings in Karl-Marx-Platz (now known again as Augustusplatz) before the Fall of the Berlin Wall, November 9th, 1989. **Buenos Aires:** The Madres de la Plaza de Mayo – The Mothers of the Plaza de Mayo – recognised by their white headscarves, were mothers who were trying to find their children who had been abducted and killed by the Argentine government of 1976–1983. Their protests (1977–2006) helped to bring about changes in the law. **New York:** The two-month occupation of Zuccotti Park in New York's financial district was a protest against social and economic inequality, and corruption and greed of big corporations and banks.

1a Vocabulary: Reasons to protest   5+ mins
people protest against: animal experiments, war, political corruption
people protest for: human rights, women's rights, worker's rights, gay rights, religious freedom, the environment

1b Our campaign   10+ mins
• Read out the first part of the instructions and play ▶ 2/11 for the gist listening.
• Then play ▶ 2/12 for the detailed listening.
The man prefers the modern protest methods.
1 W; 2 W; 3 W; 4 neither; 5 W, M; 6 M; 7 W; 8 W, M; 9 W; 10 M

(W = woman, M = man)

W: So, how are we going to get people involved in our campaign? We want to get our message to everyone. I know – let's have a demonstration in the town!

M: I don't know. Demos are OK for workers' rights and that sort of thing, but not really for our sort of campaign.

W: OK, then. What about a concert? Or even a festival, over a weekend? We could have some music and comedy. People could camp in tents. It'd be cool.

M: Cool? In the British summer? It would be more than cool, it'd be cold and wet. I'd rather not sit in a cold, wet tent for a weekend.

W: OK, what about a letter writing campaign? You can do that indoors, where it's nice and warm, if you'd rather not get cold. Letters can be very effective.

M: Sit and write letters on *paper* and put them in an *envelope* and put a *stamp* on them and *post* them in a *post box* at the end of the street? What century are we in?

W: Well, what do you suggest then? You don't want to do anything violent, do you?

M: No, of course not. It has to be a peaceful campaign.

W: Yes, absolutely.

M: I agree with you that we want to get our message to people, but I'd rather use different methods. I'd prefer to use social media – the Internet, mobile technology, that sort of thing.

W: Oh yes, we could start a petition online – an e-petition – and ask people to sign it. I've put my name to a few different e-petitions before.

M: We can do better than that. I'd prefer to start our own online campaign. We can use social media to get our message across.

W: Yes, then you can speak to a lot of people at once. That's a good way to ask people to boycott a shop, or not to buy a company's products.

M: Well, it's a lot more than that. It can be very creative. For example, you put your own video online – you know, something really clever or funny, so everyone sends it to their friends. And – another idea – we can use guerrilla techniques.

W: What do you mean?

M: We do something funny or crazy to get publicity. You know, like that protester who jumped into the water during the big Oxford and Cambridge boat race and stopped the race. He was on the television and on the front page of all the newspapers. Yes, if we do something like that, we can be in the news, too.

W: I don't know. I think I'd rather do something more … traditional. For me, there are three problems with that sort of guerrilla protest. Firstly, you can get into trouble with the police; secondly people think you're silly; and thirdly, I can remember that protester in the water, but I can't remember what he was protesting about. And our message has to be the most important thing, doesn't it?

1c	**How to express preference** 5 mins
	• Read out the phrases and have the class repeat them in chorus before students make sentences.
1d	**Now you: What would you do?** 10– mins
	• Ask the groups to make a note of any cause they all agree on. Each group should tell the class their top priority and the kind of protest they would organise.
Text	**Dear Toy Box** 5+ mins
	• Give students time to read the article to themselves and then ask: What is the 'Pink Stinks' campaign? (A campaign to stop gender-specific toys in stores.)
	• ↑ Ask students to copy and complete the sentences on the board:

She writes about gender-neutral toys, such as …	(jigsaw puzzles, board games, balls, bikes and roller skates.)
Gender-specific toys encourage boys and girls to …	(play separately.)
Hamleys has recently …	(reorganised its stores so that there isn't a separate toy department for boys and girls.)

2   **What does she say?**   10– mins
- Board: *   Underline the relevant information for questions 1 and 4 in the text.
           **   As in the coursebook.
           *** As in the coursebook. And answer: According to the text, how are some gender-neutral toys made gender-specific?

(pink skates + black or blue skates; a princess game + a pirate game; pink building bricks)

1 Toys for children are divided by gender, even the gender-neutral ones like building bricks.
2 No, not really. Toys were divided by gender in earlier generations as well, but there were also a lot of gender-neutral toys. 3 Boys and girls won't learn to work together if they don't play together. They won't know how to communicate. They will have problems in later relationships if they don't play together. We will have a more divided society. 4 Toy box should re-organise their store and not have separate departments for boys and girls. They should sell fewer gender-specific toys.

3a   **Look again**   5– mins
play | will play, have | will have

3b   **Grammar: You already know – First Conditional**   5+ mins
- Have individuals read out the sentences of the Grammar box, then ask students to write the sentences down beginning the first sentence with *They* … and the second sentence with *If* … .
! Check that students have a comma after the *if*-clause in the second sentence.
! If you want to spend longer on this point, look at the Language study explanation and exercises on page 62.

3c   **What will be the consequences?**   5+ mins
Possible answers:
1 … they'll have problems in their relationships later in life. … they won't learn how to communicate and work together. 2 … they'll learn how to work together. … they won't have problems with relationships. 3 … you'll miss your teacher. … you won't have other students to talk to. 4 … you'll meet other students and can talk to them in English. … you won't be bored.

4a   **Grammar: And now – *unless***   5 mins
- ↑ Have individuals rephrase the two sentences with *if + not*. (If you don't listen …, … / … if you don't take …)
! If you want to spend longer on this point, look at the Language study explanation and exercises on page 62.

Extra

> *Unless*   5+ mins
> - Explain that *unless* is often used for warnings. Ask students to complete these warnings to children: *Unless you eat your vegetables, … / Unless you do your homework, … / Unless you go to bed early, … / Unless you save your pocket money, … / Unless you tidy your room, … / Unless you stop eating so many sweets, … / Unless you practise the piano, … / Unless you learn your English vocabulary, … / Unless you get up early, …*

4b   **Unless you listen to us, …**   5+ mins
1 Unless you listen to parents, you'll lose a lot of customers. 2 Unless you listen to us, we'll organise a big demonstration. 3 Unless you change your plans, we'll organise a boycott. 4 I'll stop shopping in your store unless you take action. 5 We'll inform the media unless you do what we want. 6 We'll protest outside your offices unless you stop this project.

4c   **Now you choose: If I have time, …**   5+ mins
- Students choose which task they'd like to and talk to a partner – they don't need to have chosen the same task.

If short of time
- Do *Exercise 5* as a class activity, asking for a sentence from volunteers.

5   **What do you think?**   5 mins
- In class, students give their opinions on the pictures. Encourage discussion by asking follow-up questions: *Can graffiti be art? Is there graffiti in this town – where?*

Unit 3 Step 3 World Alternative Games

Contents

Text topic A ticket
Functions Talking about sport
Vocabulary Sport and sports equipment; Verbs and nouns (sport)
Grammar Focus on: *if / when*
Reading World Alternative Games

Lesson notes

www Extra activity: www.klett-langenscheidt.de/networknow/activities (Unit 3: Step 3)

Info *Theatre of dreams* (seen on the ticket) is the nickname for Old Trafford, Manchester United's football stadium, where they've played since 1910.

Starter 5 mins • Ask individual students the *Starter* questions and find out who has similar interests.

Tip: Realia (3) Personalised realia makes the lesson much more relevant. Of course, this means asking your class beforehand to bring in relevant items – photos, postcards, programmes, tickets. Only a few will remember to do so but nowadays, people often have tickets and photos on their phones. Simply asking students to take out any piece of paper from their bag – a receipt, a memo, a photo – and tell their partner about it, will produce a surprisingly lively interchange. Try it if you need to fill in five minutes at the end of a lesson.

1 **Close-up: Tickets for sporting events** 5 mins
1 Bayern Munich; 2 Block N3405; 3 N 47; 4 Row 18 Seat 101; 5 7.45pm; 6 30 minutes before kick-off (7.45pm)

2 **Sports** 10 mins
• Have three students at the board to write down the sports. Student 1 writes down the sports with *play*; Student 2 the sports with *do* and Student 3 the sports with *go*.
Possible answers: **play tennis, play basketball, go swimming, go riding, go mountain biking, go walking, go hiking, do aerobics, do judo**

3 **Vocabulary building: Verbs and nouns (sports)** 10 mins
beat an opponent, catch / hit / kick / a ball, lose a point / a match / a race, run a marathon / a race, score a goal, take part in a race / a marathon / a match, throw a ball, win a match / a marathon / a point

4a **The Olympic Games** 5 mins
This can be done as a class activity so they can pool their information.

4b Text **Reading** 10 mins
Differences: The World Alternative Games take place every two years. They don't have any traditional sports and there are no medals for the winners.
Similarities: They attract competitors from around the world. The sportsmen and sportswomen have the same motivation to win as Olympic athletes.

5 **What can you remember?** 10+ mins
• Remind the class about writing mails. Elicit how to begin a mail (Dear ...) and how to end one (Best wishes).
• Give students time to choose the event and choose a partner.

6a **Focus on ... *if / when*** 5– mins
• Read out the example sentences and the explanation in the *Focus on ...* box.

Extra

> ***if / when***   5+ mins
> * Read out the following sentences without the first word. Ask volunteers to repeat your sentence, beginning with *If* or *When*.
> (When) *the bell rings, the children will go into the playground.*
> (If) *the fire bell rings, the children will go into the playground.*
> (If) *it rains tomorrow, we won't have a picnic.*
> (If / When) *I come to the lesson next week, I'll sit in the same place.*
> (If) *I win the lottery, I'll retire.*
> (When) *I retire, I'll spend more time with my family.*
> (When) *I get home, I'll do my homework.*
> (If) *I get home early enough, I'll watch the news.*
> (When) *I go to bed, I'll set my alarm clock at 6 am.*
> (If) *I don't hear my alarm clock, I'll be late for work.*

6b **Worm charming rules**   10– mins
* Let students work in pairs to decide on the answers before asking volunteers to read out sentences to the class.

1e) If | ~~When~~, 2f) ~~if~~ | when, 3a) If | ~~When~~, 4b) if | ~~when~~, 5c) ~~If~~ | When, 6d) ~~if~~ | when

If short
of time
* Do *Exercise 7a* as a class activity.
* Choose just one event for *Exercise 7b*.

7a **Bats and balls**   5+ mins

boxing: gloves, ring; Formula 1: racing car, race track; golf: club, course; baseball: bat, field; tennis: racket, court

7b **Sporting events**   5+ mins
Possible answers:
The New York Marathon takes place every year, on the first Sunday in November. It didn't take place in 2012 because of Hurricane Sandy.
The Fifa World Cup is the most important football game and it takes place every four years. The winner is the world champion and gets the Jules Rimet Trophy.
The Ryder Cup is a golf game between the UK and the US. It takes place every two years.
Wimbledon, in London, hosts the oldest tennis tournament in the world (since 1887).
The America's Cup is the most famous competitive sailing race.

8 **What do you think?**   5+ mins
* Class discussion prompted by the quotation. If necessary, ask follow-up questions, e.g. *What can be done to stop football hooliganism?*

Unit 3 Now I can

Contents   Review of vocabulary, functions and structures in Unit 3

Lesson notes

www   You can download and copy a **Project sheet** to be used for the writing activities in *Now I can*: www.klett-langenscheidt.de/networknow/activities (Unit 3: Now I can)

Now I can:
...
5 mins • Ask students to look at *Now I can: ...* at the top of page 68. Remind them that the symbols refer to different skills or vocabulary items they learnt in Unit 3 and were listed in the unit aims on p. 53.

Starter   **Saying how and why people protest; Talking about sport**   10– mins

Look back

Possible answers: **lendwithcare.org: It's a charity organisation which gives loans / lends money to poor people funding their business ideas and helping them to work their way out of poverty. PinkStinks.org.UK: It's an organisation which is against the 'pinkification' of girls' lives by pink toys. Wales 2012: It's the organisation which creates the World Alternative Games in 2012.**

Now look forward

• Ask why companies sponsor people. (It's good for their image.)

Part 1 **Describing a business**

What does your company do? 10 mins
! If you have downloaded and copied the Project sheet, you can use it for this exercise, *Exercise 2a, 2c and 4.*

Part 2 **Talking about plans, intentions and decisions; Expressing preference; Talking about sport**

2a **Three sports** 10+ mins
• You can use the Project sheet for this exercise.

2b **Three sports stars of tomorrow** 10+ mins
• Read out the first part of the instructions and play ▶ 2/19.
2/19–20 • Read out the second part of the instructions and play ▶ 2/20.

Name, age: <u>Ashton</u>, 17; Sport: golf; Achievements: has won three major junior competitions, has already played on some of the most famous golf courses in the world; Aims: to become a professional golfer, to take his place on the senior tour, to win one of the major tournaments on one of the famous golf courses in the world, to become a star of tomorrow; Notes: His dad is his coach.

Name, age: <u>Jade</u>, 16; Sport: basketball; Achievements: her team came third in the under 17s championships last year; Aims: to play at an international level, to be in the team for the Olympics, wants to go to America next summer for a training programme, plans to study sports science at university; Notes: Her mum's British and her dad's from Hungary, so she could play for either country.

Name, age: <u>Max</u>, 17; Sport: Boxing; Achievements: was second in the national championships; Aims: to take part in the Olympics, to win in the national championships next month; Notes: He wants to make his team and his family proud of him. He wants to be a good role model. He thinks that boxing keeps you off the streets and gives you something positive to do with your energy.

Ashton:	Hi. My name's Ashton. I'm 17 and I'm a golfer. I travel round the world on the junior tour circuit. Last year I won three major junior competitions. As soon as I'm 18, I'm going to become a professional golfer and take my place on the senior tour. My dad – he's my coach too – he thinks I can make it really big. I've already played on some of the most famous golf courses in the world – St Andrews in Scotland, Augusta in the USA and Royal Melbourne in Australia – and I'm going to win one of the major tournaments there one day. Right now, I'm looking for sponsorship to help with my travel costs. This is a great opportunity for a company to sponsor one of the stars of tomorrow.
Jade:	Hi. My name's Jade. I'm from London. I'm 16 years old and I play basketball for my school team. After the 2012 Olympics in London, some of the athletes and coaches of all sorts of different sports came to our school and that's how I got involved. They saw that I was tall and suggested basketball. Last year our team came third in our age category – that's the under 17s – in the UK championships. But our coach thinks I can play at an international level. My mum's British and my dad's from Hungary, so I could play for either country. Of course my dream is to be in the team for the Olympics – that would be amazing. I intend to achieve that. I'm looking for sponsorship because I've got the chance to go to America next summer for a special training programme. I'm also planning to study sports science at university – and to continue with basketball at the same time, of course.
Max:	I'm Max. I'm a middleweight boxer and I've been involved in boxing since my 11th birthday, when my granddad took me to our local boxing club. He was a keen amateur boxer when he was my age. My coach thinks I've got the potential to take part in the Olympics. I've got an injury at the moment, but my whole team – my coach, our team doctor and the physiotherapists – are working hard to make sure I'm fit for the national championships next month. I came second there last year, so I plan to win this time. I want to make my team and my family proud of me. And I intend to be a good role model for younger boys – boxing keeps you off the streets and gives you something positive to do with your energy. It'd be great to have some sponsorship to help with my training costs, so thanks for your interest.

2c	**Who shall we sponsor?** 10+ mins

• You can use the Project sheet for this exercise.

Part 3	**Talking about plans, intentions and decisions; Saying how and why people protest**

3a	**A protest** 5 mins

- ↓ Give prompts if necessary: *Where are the sports clothes made? / Who works in the factories that make them? / What are they made of?*

  Board: trainers and T-shirts
  Bangladesh
  factory conditions
  child workers
  boycott

If short of time	• Do **Exercise 3b** as a class activity, with students from each group volunteering information.

3b	**Two protests** 10 mins

Tip: Prompts It's helpful to weaker students to have prompts for discussions. If you think your class will find an activity challenging, you can write prompts on the board (see above). But if you know that one or two students might need support, prepare slips of papers with prompts on them which you can give discreetly to weaker students. For example, for *Exercise 3b*:

Student A:
sports firm – factory in Indonesia – long hours – dangerous conditions – fire – 3 workers – boycott – press conference

Student B:
factory in China – petition – 200,000 signatures – working conditions – sports shoes – child labour – million signatures

- Before doing the pairwork activity, divide the class into A and B groups and let them read and discuss their texts in the group.
- Then put them into A/B pairs and let them talk about the protests.
- Finally, have a class vote to see which protest would be the more effective.

4	**Now you choose** 10 mins

- You can use the Project sheet for this exercise.
- Remind students about the star system and tell them they can choose one of the tasks.
- Students find people who want to do the same task and they work together.

And finally	5 mins • Look back at the *In this unit, you will learn to: ...* (p. 53) to show your students how much they have learnt in this unit and say how well they've done.

- Remind students about the homework pages for this lesson – the *Test yourself* pages (pp. 70/71).
- If you don't plan to use the extra pages (*English worldwide*, *English at work* and *Story*) in the lesson, students can enjoy these pages at home.

Unit 4 Step 1 Is it safe?

Contents

Text topic An article about safety
Functions Comparing things; Understanding operating instructions
Vocabulary Parts of an electrical appliance
Grammar **You already know:** Comparison (1) – comparatives and superlatives
And now: Comparison (2) – degrees of comparison

Lesson notes

www **Extra activity:** www.klett-langenscheidt.de/networknow/activities (Unit 4: Step 1)

Starter 5+ mins • Ask individual students the *Starter* questions.

1 **What's dangerous?** 5+ mins
• After five minutes, ask volunteers for their answers – stress there is no right or wrong.
Possible answers: 1 pilot, police officer 2 Driving is more dangerous as there are more car accidents than plane crashes. 3 A swimming pool is more dangerous as little children can fall into it and drown. 4 The kitchen is the most dangerous room – it has a hot cooker and sharp knives. 5 A hair dryer can be dangerous if it falls into water. A toaster and the cooker could be dangerous as they could get too hot.

Text **Risk – and how we see it** 10 mins
• ↑ Ask volunteers to add one more sentence to each section.

2a **Look again** 5– mins
Sentence 1 compares two things. Sentence 2 looks at one item in a whole category.

2b **Grammar: You already know – Comparison (1)** 5+ mins
• Focus attention on the Grammar box and read out the sentences. Write these ways of travelling on the board: travelling ... by car / by train / by bus / by air / by motorbike / by scooter
• Ask volunteers to make similar sentences about those ways of travelling.
! For more explanations and practice, you can look at the Language study on page 79.

3a **Grammar: And now – Comparison (2)** 5+ mins
• Read out the sentences in the Grammar box.
• Ask volunteers to make similar sentences about ways of travelling with the adjective *nice*.
• Ask them to make similar sentences about ways of travelling with the adjective *convenient*.
! For more explanations and practice, you can look at the Language study on page 79.

Extra
> **Comparison** 10– mins
> • Give statements as prompts and ask volunteers to make comparative sentences, e.g.
> Prompt: *Russian is difficult.*
> Student: *Chinese is a lot more difficult than Russian. / It isn't quite as difficult as Chinese.*
> (Possible prompts: *Motor racing is interesting. / My bag is very heavy. / Biographies are quite interesting. / Jogging is healthy. / Snowboarding is really easy. / Mexican food is hot. / Train tickets are expensive.*)

3b **More or less?** 10 mins

Tip: Reinforcement If you have a weak class, do some of the pairwork activities as class activities so that students get aural reinforcement of the structure. Ask the more able students to answer first until the weaker students have digested the structure, then make sure that everyone has had a chance to do the activity.

• Encourage students to use the phrases from *Exercise 3a*.
• Board: * Make sentences with *safe* and *dangerous*.
    ** As in coursebook.
    *** Do the activity, then write a sentence of your own with each adjective.

3c   **Now you: Your safety**   5+ mins
- Monitor group discussion, interact, and encourage shy students.

4a   **Vocabulary: Parts of an electrical appliance**   5 mins
lamp: cable, plug; radio: display, handle; TV set: screen, button, dial

4b   **A new appliance**   5 mins
2/27
- Read out the instruction and play ▶ 2/27.

It's a (tumble) dryer.

> (M = man, W = woman)
> W: Right, are we ready? Let's plug it in and turn it on!
> M: Well, just wait a moment. Let's check the instructions first. I've got them here. 'Connect the appliance to the power supply'.
> W: That's what I said – plug it in and turn it on! OK. That's on now. And I'll put the clothes in.
> M: Next, the instructions say, 'Select the desired programme'. OK, so, do you want to do that? Choose the programme you want.
> W: Right. Let me see … what do we want? 'Cottons and colours, mixed, synthetics, quick dry' … er, OK 'mixed' I think. And do we want 'iron dry' or 'cupboard dry'?
> M: What's the difference?
> W: Well, I guess 'cupboard dry' is totally dry, so you can just put the clothes straight from the machine into your cupboard, and 'iron dry' is so the clothes aren't so dry and are easier to iron. 'Cupboard dry', I think. Right, I'll start the machine.
> M: Nothing's happening.
> W: No. What's the matter? Oh, hold on, let's check the door is closed. Ah, that's it!
> M: Yes, there's a warning here in the instructions: 'Ensure that the door is fully closed'. It must be a common problem. And there's one last instruction: 'After use, disconnect from the power supply'.
> W: What? Turn it off and unplug it when you've finished? Do they mean you should take the plug out every time? That's not very realistic.
> M: No, we'll probably just turn the dryer off and leave it connected to the power.
> W: Yes, right. But isn't it great to have a tumble dryer at last? It'll be so useful in the winter.

If short of time
- Omit the second listening in *Exercise 5a*.
- Do *Exercise 6* as a class activity with just one phrase: *I (don't) feel safe when …*

5a   **What are the instructions?**   10 mins
2/28
- After students have done the matching exercise, play ▶ 2/28.

1 a) Instructions b) Everyday, 2 a) Instructions b) Everyday, 3 a) Everyday b) Instructions, 4 a) Everyday b) Instructions

Audio script: see track 2/27 above.

5b   **How to understand operating instructions**   5 mins
- Have volunteers read out and complete the sentences – refer them to *Exercise 5a* for some ideas.

5c   **Which machine?**   5 mins
NB PIN = Personal Identification Number; ATM = Automated Teller Machine (cash machine)
1d), 2c), 3e), 4b), 5a)

6   **What do you think?**   5+ mins
- Students work in groups of 3 or 4 and complete the phrases and discuss the topics.

Unit 4 Step 2 Grow your own food

Contents

Text topic Journal entries about self-sufficiency
Functions Talking about experiences; Talking about food and production; Expressing interest and indifference
Vocabulary Current issues
Grammar **You already know:** Present perfect / past simple
And now: *been / gone*

Lesson notes

www **Extra activity:** www.klett-langenscheidt.de/networknow/activities (Unit 4: Step 2)

Starter 5 mins • ! Answers may vary from: my garden, the local shop, a big supermarket, Italy, …

1 **Fresh food** 5+ mins
! Remind students that we talk about what we *have done* for things that have happened at some time in our lives – that's why the questionnaire uses *have done* (present perfect).
When we talk about a specific time or event in the past, we use *did* (past simple), e.g. *I've done a lot of self-sufficiency courses. I did one last summer.*
• Make sure the students use the past simple tense when they ask for details of the experiences.

2a **Look again** 5 mins
Q1: an experience in your life. Q2 and Q3: details about one specific time.

2b **Grammar: You already know – Present perfect / past simple** 5 mins
• Have individuals read out the sentences.
! If you want to spend longer on this point, look at the Language study explanation and exercises on page 84.

2c **Now you: Your experiences with foreign food** 5 mins
• ↓ If students need prompting, ask: *Where was your last / most exotic holiday? What's a typical food or drink in that country?* And write some examples on the board.

Text **Tip: Reading skills (6)** The questions on the texts are gradually changing from 'right / wrong' answers to discussion questions. But a few comprehension questions after the first reading will support weaker students.

Maggie's self-sufficiency journal 10 mins
• Give students time to read the journal entries to themselves and then ask individuals to complete the sentences about each paragraph.
Board:

1 Maggie and Ian have read a lot of info about …	(self-sufficiency)
2 They've already done …	(a lot of work in the garden)
3 Yesterday Maggie went …	(to a lake and picked some blackberries)
4 Ian has gone …	(to the woods with the children)
5 Maggie's become …	(involved in community food production)
6 Ian's been …	(to a house with a wood-burning oven)

3 **Do you agree?** 5+ mins
Possible answers: **1** No – they've been interested in the idea of self-sufficiency for a long time. **2** You can't really tell that at the moment as they've just started, but they've got a lot of good ideas. **3** Yes – their children are allowed to do dangerous things: go to the woods alone, climb trees, collect wild mushrooms and eat them. **4** Yes – she cut her foot when she was working in the garden because she was just wearing sandals and her arms were scratched when she picked some fruits at a lake because she wasn't wearing something with long sleeves. **5** No – Maggie has become involved in the community food production.
6 Yes – we hear of Ian going to the garden centre / the woods / the pub / to Hungerford.

4a   **Grammar: And now – *been / gone***   5 mins
- Read out the first sentence and ask: *Is he still at the house?* (No.)
- Read out the second sentence and ask: *Is he still at the garden centre?* (Yes.)

! If you want to spend longer on this point, look at the Language study explanation and exercises on page 84.

Extra

> ***been / gone***   5 mins
> - Get students to respond to your prompts with *Where* – questions with *been* and *gone*.
>   *My sister's on holiday.* (Where's she gone?) *To Thailand.*
>   *My brother has just come back.* (Where's he been?) *To Austria.*
>   *My boss isn't here.* (Where's he gone?) *To a meeting.*
>   *James left a few minutes ago.* (Where's he gone?) *To the airport.*
>   *Petra is really sunburnt.* (Where's she been?) *To India.*
>   *I've just come back* (Where have you been?) *To the bank.*
>   *They took off at 9.20.* (Where've they gone?) *To Paris.*

4b   **Now you: Where have you been?**   5+ mins
! 1 requires the use of *been*; 2 requires the use of *gone*.

5a   **Vocabulary: Current issues**   5+ mins
- Students listen and repeat when you play ▶ 2/33.
- Then they discuss current news.

2/33

If short of time
- Omit the first task in *Exercise 5b*.
- Just look at the second photo in *Exercise 6*.

5b   **What's the problem?**   10+ mins
- Read out the first instruction and play ▶ 2/34.

2/34–35

climate change, the environment, food production, the economic situation, unemployment
- Then play ▶ 2/35.

✓ **concerned about, involved in, bothered about, worry about**

(N1 = neighbour 1, N2 = neighbour 2)
N1: Morning! Lovely day, isn't it?
N2: Yes, it's good to see the sun. What *is* happening with the weather at the moment?
N1: Yes, we had a lot of rain in the summer, and it was so cold. And now there's this warm autumn. Scientists say that the whole world is getting warmer.
N2: Yes, the experts are really concerned about it. What *are* we doing to our environment?!
N1: I was talking to a farmer at the market last week – I was buying some apples – and *she* said they'd had a very bad year.
N2: Was that the farmers market?
N1: Yes, I try to buy locally produced fruit and veg when I can …
N2: Oh yes, you're involved in the campaign for people to buy locally produced food, aren't you?
N1: That's right. It's going really well. We've had a good response from local people. They always think it'll be more expensive to buy local food, but it can be cheaper.
N2: Really? That's interesting. To be honest, I'm not so bothered about where my food comes from, if it's cheap.
N1: Well, we *all* have to be careful with money at the moment. A lot of people have money problems. Did you hear that Jim – you know Jim – Jim and Carol at number 3 – he lost his job last week?
N2: No, I didn't. It's happening to a lot of people. And young people can't find a first job. Times are hard.
N1: Yes, I worry about *my* job sometimes. Oh, goodness – my job, yes, oh dear – I'm going to be late for work! I must run! Bye!
N2: Bye! I hope you get there on time!

5c   **How to express interest and indifference**   5 mins
- Have individuals read out the phrases, completing them in their own way.

5d
Now you: How do you feel about it? 5 mins
- Monitor the activity, joining in and prompting where necessary.

5e
Now you choose: Your priorities 5 mins
- Students work in pairs and it doesn't matter if they each choose a different task.

6
What do you think? 5 mins
- In class, students give their opinions on the three pictures. Encourage discussion by asking follow-up questions: *What's the difference between vegan and vegetarian?* (vegetarians don't eat meat; vegans don't eat or use animal products, like leather or honey or milk) *What does 'vegan friendly' mean?* (contains no animal products) *What problems might vegans have?* (difficult to find vegan products or vegan dishes in restaurants / non-leather clothes)

Unit 4 Step 3 Superstition

Contents

Text topic A fortune cookie
Functions Explaining things in your own words
Vocabulary Synonyms; Superstitions; Adjectives ending in *-ing / -ed*
Grammar Focus on: Adjectives ending in *-ing / -ed*
Reading Australia's hidden shoes

Lesson notes

www **Extra activity:** www.klett-langenscheidt.de/networknow/activities (Unit 4: Step 3)

Starter 5 mins • Ask individual students the *Starter* questions.

1a
Close-up: Fortune cookies 5 mins
Possible answer: **It's good to listen to others. You can learn from people's mistakes and experiences.**

1b
I think it means ... 5 mins

Tip: Realia (4) It takes time to build up a useful collection of classroom realia so always be on the lookout for adverts in English-language magazines, newspaper headlines, tickets, programmes, menus, holiday brochures, etc. But remember that German sources can also be used. For example, you could copy horoscopes from a German magazines and let students ask each other when their birthday is and give a gist translation of their partner's horoscope.

NB *Will* is normally used for predictions.
Possible answers:
A stranger will present you with a gift. – It says that you will get a present from a person you don't know.
A face from the past will re-enter your life. – I think it means that you will meet a person you knew when you were younger and he / she will play a role in your life again.
You will receive an offer you cannot refuse. –I think it means that there will be an opportunity which is so good that you can't say no to it.

2 Text
Reading 10+ mins
- Give students about eight minutes to read the article and to talk to others / to you if anything is unclear.
They put shoes in buildings, e.g. behind walls, up chimneys and under floors and roofs.

3a
Vocabulary building: Synonyms 10+ mins
- Have students underline the words 1–8 in the text and read out the sentences containing them, so that you're sure everyone has found the words.
- Give students time to do the exercise and then check the answers by having volunteers read out the sentences, replacing the underlined words with words a) to h).
7a), 5b), 4c), 6d), 1e), 8f), 2g), 3h)

3b   **In other words**   5 mins
Possible answers:
- An unusual find in Australia has <u>revealed</u> that some people were still practising a very old superstition in the early 20th century.
- While workmen were repairing the Sydney Harbour Bridge, which was <u>constructed</u> in the 1920s, they <u>discovered</u> a child's shoe hidden in the bridge.
- The practice of <u>concealing</u> shoes in houses and other buildings for protection is a superstition which began in Europe in the Middle Ages.
- They were <u>terrified</u> of evil spirits.
- Recently in a house in Tasmania, historians were <u>amazed</u> to find forty shoes.
- In the 18th and 19th centuries, there was no real health care and children often died young because they didn't <u>receive</u> the necessary medical treatment.
- Parents were very <u>concerned</u> about their children's health and safety.

4   **What can you remember?**   10 mins
- Board: *   Look back at the text.
              **   As in coursebook.
              ***   Write as many facts as you can in the given time.
- Stop the writing after five minutes and use the next five minutes for the question and answer phase.

5a   **Focus on ...** *if / when*   5 mins
- Read out the sentences and explanation in the box.

Extra
> **Adjectives ending in** *-ing / -ed*   10– mins
> - Board: I was (bored) because the speaker was so (boring).
>   Ask the class: *How did you feel – and why?* Then read out the prompts:
>
> | | |
> |---|---|
> | The lesson was so interesting. | The story was so fascinating. |
> | The game was so exciting. | The exam results were so amazing. |
> | The horror film was so terrifying. | The news was so surprising. |
> | The storm was so frightening. | The ski tour was so tiring. |

5b   **It's fascinating!**   5 mins
1 ~~fascinated~~ | fascinating 2 interested | ~~interesting~~ 3 ~~surprised~~ | surprising 4 ~~terrified~~ | terrifying
5 frightened | ~~frightening~~

If short of time
- Omit the second stage of *Exercise 5b*.
- Do *Exercise 6b* as a class activity with volunteers from the A / B groups.

6a   **British superstitions**   5+ mins
4, 5, 1, 3, 2, 7, 6
(Good luck: 1, 2, 5; Bad luck: 3, 4, 6, 7)

6b   **Good luck and bad luck**   10+ mins
- Divide the class into two groups, A and B. Give them time to read their texts and help each other with the meanings before putting them into A/B pairs to do the activity.

6c   **Now you: Superstitions in your country**   5+ mins
- Focus on non-German members of the class, to add variety and interest.
  Answers vary from country to country, e.g. in Germany, people hold their thumbs to wish you luck.

7   **What do you think?**   5+ mins
- Class discussion prompted by the quotation. If necessary, ask follow-up questions, e.g. *What 'lucky breaks' have you had in your professional life / social life?*

Unit 4 Now I can

Contents	Review of vocabulary, functions and structures in Unit 4

Lesson notes

www   You can download and copy a **Project sheet** to be used for the writing activities in *Now I can*: www.klett-langenscheidt.de/networknow/activities (Unit 4: Now I can)

Now I can: ...   5 mins • Ask students to look at *Now I can: ...* at the top of page 90. Remind them that the symbols refer to different skills or vocabulary items they learnt in Unit 4 and were listed in the unit aims on p. 75.

Starter   **Comparing things**   10– mins

Look back

Possible answers: **The mushroom could cause the most serious accident. You could be ill or die if you eat some kinds of mushrooms. Buy a book about which mushrooms are safe to eat.**

Now look forward   • Ask what kind of street food you can buy locally.

Part 1   **Talking about food production; Expressing interest and indifference**

What are you concerned about?   5+ mins
• After the group discussion, have a show of hands to find out the most common statement.

Part 2   **Comparing things; Talking about experiences**

2a   **Street food around the world**   10+ mins
! If you have downloaded and copied the Project sheet, you can use it for this activity and for *Exercise 2c* and *3a*.

Possible answers: **Turkey – doner kebab, börek, köfte | Greece – gyros, tzatziki | India – curry, pappadums | Thailand – phat thai (rice noodles), tom kha gai | the UK – fish and chips, roast beef | the USA – burgers, French fries, hot dogs, donuts | Poland – zapiekanki, obwarzanki, precle, lody | Germany – sausages, Sauerkraut, Apfelstrudel**

2b   **Which snack would be best?**   5+ mins
• Follow coursebook instructions.

2c   **Market research**   10 mins
• You can use the Project sheet for this exercise.

2/41–42

Tip: Setting up listenings (3) It can make the listening task easier if you pause two or three times during the first listening. This gives students time to write down any notes they may need and takes away the common fear of: *It'll be too fast and I won't understand it.*

• Read out the first part of the instructions and play ▶ 2/41, pausing the CD after each section (where you see ^^^ in the audio script on the next page).
• Play the interview again ▶ 2/42, and pause the CD to give students time to write.

Börek: A good snack because it's quick. It's little parcels filled with meat or cheese. He's eaten it in a restaurant in Turkey. **Falafel:** A good snack because it's healthy. He's eaten it a couple of times, e.g. at a music festival last summer – at a Lebanese stall. It's served in pitta bread, with salad. **Currywurst:** He's never eaten it but curry and chips is a good combination – so why not put a sausage in there, too?

Five questions that the researcher asks:
Have you ever tried börek?
Did you eat them in a restaurant or in the street?
Have you ever eaten falafel?
How were they served?
Have you ever heard of currywurst?

➡

(MR = market researcher, MS = man in the street)

MR: Excuse me, I'd like to ask you a couple of questions – if you have a moment.

MS: OK.

MR: I'm going to ask you about different street food – different types of snacks that you can buy to eat in the street. So, first – have you ever tried börek?

MS: Oh, those little parcel things filled with spicy meat?

MR: That's right – and you can get cheese ones, too.

MS: Yes, I've eaten those. I went to Turkey on holiday last summer and we ate a lot of interesting spicy things, including börek.

MR: Did you eat them in a restaurant or in the street?

MS: Both, I think. Yes, both. They're only small, so they're very good as a quick snack.

∧∧∧

MR: Right. And – next one – have you ever eaten falafel?

MS: Yes, I have. I go to a lot of music festivals and they have all sorts of different food from around the world. There was a good Lebanese stall at the World Music Festival last summer, so I ate falafel a couple of times there.

MS: How were they served?

MS: In pitta bread, with salad – like a doner kebab. It's a good healthy snack – better than chips, anyway.

∧∧∧

MR: OK. And – last question – have you ever heard of currywurst?

MS: Curry what?

MR: Currywurst. It's a popular snack in Germany. Its name means 'curry sausage' and it's a sausage served with a curry sauce, like a spicy ketchup. And you usually have chips with it.

MS: Oh, right. No, I've never heard of it, but it sounds like a good combination. Chips with curry sauce is a popular snack here, so why not put a sausage in there too?

MR: OK, well thanks very much for your time.

MS: You're welcome. Bye.

2d   **Have you ever eaten …?**   10 mins
- Follow coursebook instructions.

Part 3   **Understanding operating instructions; Explaining things in your own words**

If short   • Do *Exercise 3a* as a class activity, with volunteers reading out an instruction to the other group.
of time   • Do *Exercise 3b* as a class activity.

3a   **Operating instructions**   5 mins
- You can use the Project sheet for this exercise.
- Divide the class into A and B groups. Let them complete the operating instructions together before getting them to work as A/B partners.
  Partner A – juice machine: Plug, Turn, Put, Check, Press, Disconnect
  Partner B – toaster: in, dial, down, up, power

3b   **Keep it clean**   10 mins
Possible answers:
1 Don't put food which isn't cooked and food which is cooked next to each other.
2 Don't take the food out of the fridge before you really need it.
3 Clean the table you're working on between the different things you do.
4 Make sure that the 'use by' dates on all packaged food are OK.
5 If an employee gets ill, tell your manager immediately.

4   **Now you choose**   10 mins
- Remind students about the star system and tell them they can choose one of the tasks.
- Students find people who want to do the same task and they work together.

And finally   5 mins   • Look back at the *In this unit, you will learn to: …* (p. 75) to show your students how much they have learnt in this unit and say how well they've done.
- Remind students about the homework pages for this lesson – the *Test yourself* pages (pp. 92/93).
- If you don't plan to use the extra pages (*English worldwide* and *English at work*) in the lesson, students can enjoy these pages at home

Unit 5 Step 1 False alarm

Contents

Text topic   Two newspaper articles
Functions   Dealing with problems when travelling
Vocabulary   Travel problems
Grammar   Reported speech 1 (statements – present simple)

Lesson notes

www   **Extra activity:** www.klett-langenscheidt.de/networknow/activities (Unit 5: Step 1)

Starter   5+ mins • Ask individual students the *Starter* questions.
Possible answers: **bad weather conditions, problems with the plane('s engine), no pilot, terrorism**

Tip: Reading skills (7) When dealing with divided texts, split the class into groups and let each group read one text and then relate the content to the other group(s) before giving the class a chance to read the remaining texts. This is a good test of comprehension and of the ability to rephrase information.

Text   **Stop the plane … / Immigration officer …**   10+ mins

Tip: Reading skills (7) When dealing with divided texts, split the class into groups and let each group read one text and then relate the content to the other group(s) before giving the class a chance to read the remaining texts. This is a good test of comprehension and of the ability to rephrase information.

- Divide the class into A/B groups.
- Group A reads the first article while Group B reads the second one.
- Without referring to their books, ask volunteers from Group A to tell Group B about the first article. Then do the same with Group B.
- Have the groups read the article they were told about.

1a   **What did they do?**   5+ mins
- Students from the two groups make A/B pairs and do the task.
I wanted to fly to Morocco to get married. My mother phoned security at the airport and told them I was a terrorist, so the take-off was delayed. I was really angry!
I put my wife's name on a list of terrorists so she couldn't return to the UK from Pakistan. I just wanted to be single again so I didn't want her to come back!

1b   **Who said it?**   5 mins
1 the 56-year-old woman / mother, 2 the mother's lawyer, 3 the mother's lawyer, 4 security officers at the airport in Pakistan, 5 the woman's husband, 6 the woman's husband

2a   **Grammar: Reported speech 1 (statements – present simple)**   5+ mins
- Focus attention on the Grammar box and read out the direct speech sentences. Have volunteers read out the conversion into reported speech.
- Point out that when the 'saying' verb *(said, repeated, explained, promised)* is in the past tense, the following verbs must also be in the past tense.
- Refer students to the Info box: *tell* is followed by a person.
! For more explanations and practice, you can look at the Language study on page 101.

Extra
    Reported speech 1 (statements – present simple)   5+ mins
    - Say a sentence in the present tense and elicit two reported speech sentences – with *said* and *told*.
    - Board: He / She said that …   He / She told us that …
    Prompts:
    I'm tired. I'm hungry. I'm cold. I'm late. (She said / told us that she was …)
    The children are very nice. They are friendly. They are polite. They aren't loud. They are teenagers.
    They're not at school, they're on holiday. (She said / told us that they were / weren't …)
    I have a cold. I have a new phone. I have no time. I don't have enough time. I don't have any children.
    I have an English DVD. I don't have wine. (She said / told us that she had / didn't have …)

2b **What did he say?** 5+ mins
- Do this as a class activity so that you can check that the concept has been understood.
  He said (that) / He told them (that) …
  1 … life was great. 2 … he went out every night. 3 … his wife phoned him from Pakistan every week.
  4 … he didn't want her back.

2c **Good news or bad news?** 5+ mins
They said (that) / They told me (that) … 1 … the flight was delayed. (bad news); 2 … the airport was closed … (bad news); 3 … there were free drinks … (good news); 4 … my flight was overbooked. (bad news); 5 … my flight wasn't ready … (bad news); 6 … the pilots were on strike. (bad news); 7 … they had a small technical problem. (bad news); 8 … they didn't have my booking … (bad news); 9 … my luggage was booked through … (good news); 10 … the toilets were out of order. (bad news)

3a **Vocabulary: Travel problems** 10– mins
! Follow the instructions carefully – we don't want students to use reported speech here as it would lead them to using the past perfect tense! Write on the board: When (Beate) went on holiday, …

3b **Good customer service?** 10– mins
- Read out the first part of the instructions and play ▶ 3/2.
- Play the conversations again ▶ 3/3. Pause the CD between the dialogues so the students can write the questions.
  1 Problem: The guest's room isn't ready. – The receptionist gives good customer service as he gives a possible reason for this, offers coffee in the lounge and says he'll tell the guest how long it will take as soon as he knows.
  2 Problem: The guest misunderstood 'bathroom' and expected a room with a bath but his room has only got a shower. – The receptionist doesn't give very good service. He offers a different room with a bath but only for a different tariff.
  Questions:
  Guest 1: How long will it take?
  Guest 2: Can I speak to the manager?

(G1 = guest 1, R1 = receptionist 1, G2 = guest 2, R2 = receptionist 2)
1
G1: Excuse me.
R1: Yes, can I help you?
G1: Yes, I have a problem. I checked in about two minutes ago and I've just been to my room, but the room isn't ready. Or maybe it's the wrong room.
R1: What room number do you have?
G1: 402. And my name is Rafael, R-A-F-A-E-L.
R1: OK, let's see … Ah yes, Mr Rafael, the computer system has you in room 402. That's correct. It must be a problem with the cleaning staff. I'll phone the housekeeping department and sort it out. While you're waiting, would you like to take a seat in the lounge? There's coffee in there.
G1: OK, I can do that. But – how long will it take?
R1: I'm not sure, but I'll let you know as soon as I have information.

2
G2: Excuse me, I have a problem.
R2: Oh, what's the matter?
G2: I checked in about five minutes ago and I've just been up to my room, but it's the wrong room.
R2: What do you mean?
G2: I booked a room with a bathroom but there isn't a bath, there's only a shower.
R2: Oh, I see. Well, 'bathroom' doesn't really mean that there has to be a bath. Some of our bathrooms have baths, some have showers.
G2: But I don't want a shower, I want a bath.
R2: OK, let me look on the computer and see if I can find one for you.
G2: Thank you.
R2: Yes, we have a room with a bath. But I'm afraid it's a different tariff. It's a deluxe room, so it's more expensive.
G2: Oh dear. Can I speak to the manager?
R2: Yes, of course, I'll call her for you.

3c   **How to deal with travel problems**   5– mins
- Read out the phrases.

If short of time
- Do *Exercise 3d* as a class activity, asking for responses from volunteers.

3d   **I have a problem**   10– mins
- Put the class into A/B pairs and monitor the activity, giving help where necessary.
  - R: The wrong room? What do you mean?
  - R: Oh dear, I'm sorry about that. Have you got your booking confirmation?
  - R: Yes, I see that you're right. It must be a mistake.
  - R: Let's find you a better room. Yes, room 102 is free. Here's the key.
  - R: You're welcome. Enjoy your stay.

  - GS: Where are you flying to?
  - GS: It's only a short delay. There's a small technical problem, but the crew are dealing with it now.
  - GS: Not long. We hope to start boarding in 30 minutes.
  - GS: No, you should be fine. Your luggage is booked through to New York, so there won't be a problem.
  - GS: You're welcome. Have a good flight.

3e   **Now you choose: A travel problem you had**   5+ mins
- Students choose which task they'd like to do and talk to a partner who has chosen the same task.

4   **What do you think?**   5 mins
- In class, students give their opinions on the pictures. Encourage discussion by asking follow-up questions: *What was the last flight you were on? What services did they offer? What's the difference between economy and business class? Which airline do you like most / least? Why?*

Unit 5 Step 2 Storybook Dads

Contents

Text topic   An article about the organisation Storybook Dads
Functions   Talking about books; Talking about communication technology
Vocabulary   Communication technology; Types of books
Grammar   Reported speech 2 (orders and requests)

Lesson notes

www   Extra activity: www.klett-langenscheidt.de/networknow/activities (Unit 5: Step 2)

Info   Students can learn more about the organisation by typing *Storybook Dads* into their search engine.

Starter   5 mins • Ask individual students the *Starter* question.

1a   **Are you a bookworm?**   5+ mins
- Ask volunteers to read out statements which apply to them.

Communication | Step 2 | Storybook Dads

1b

3/9–10

Three books 10+ mins
- Read out the first part of the instructions and play ▶ 3/9.
- ↓ Board:

1 Historical crime story: The _____ in the Thames
2 Short stories / Travel: The _____ road
3 Autobiography: Groucho and _____

- Read out the second part of the instructions and play ▶ 3/10.
  historical crime story – 'The Body in the Thames', short story – 'The White Road and Other Stories', autobiography – 'Groucho and Me'

(P = presenter, G = guest / Mark Thornton)

P: Here in the studio with me this afternoon I have Mark Thornton from the bookshop in Abingdon called Mostly Books. Hi Mark.

G: Hello.

P: Maybe you're looking for a gift for someone, or something to read yourself. Mark's got some tips for us. So, what's your first book?

G: The first one I'd like to recommend today is called 'The Body in the Thames'.

P: 'The Body in the Thames' – it sounds like a crime story.

G: Yes, it is. It's the latest book in a series of crime stories by Susanna Gregory and it takes place in London in 1664.

P: So it's a historical crime story?

G: Yes, you get a really good idea of what it was like to live in London in the 17th century. The writer knows a lot about the history of the city and about how people lived in those days. And it's a great story. An exciting mystery with a lot of clever clues. I'd recommend it if you like detective stories as it's just a little bit different.

P: Sounds good. What's next?

G: My next recommendation for you is a book of short stories.

P: Oh, I like short stories. They're great when you don't have much time to read.

G: Yes, some of the stories in here are only two or three pages long, but they're very well written. It's called 'The White Road and Other Stories' by Tania Hershman. The 'white road' in the title

is in Antarctica, and all of the stories are set in fascinating places around the world. And there are a lot of interesting ideas about science in there, too, so it's very informative. If you like reading about interesting places in the world and you're interested in scientific ideas, then I'd recommend this book.

P: Travel and science? My dad would like that.

G: Well, you should buy it for him! And my last recommendation today is a very old book. It was written in 1959.

P: Good to know you're giving us all the latest tips, Mark!

G: Well, my excuse is that I wasn't even born in 1959, so I couldn't read it then. But I've just read it and it's excellent.

P: So, what is it?

G: It's the autobiography of Groucho Marx.

P: Oh, Groucho from the Marx brothers? The one with the big black moustache and the big fat cigar?

G: Yes, he was a really big name in Hollywood.

P: I love the old Marx brothers films. They're so funny, even today.

G: Yes, and this book is very funny, too, as you can imagine. Honestly, I couldn't stop laughing when I was reading it.

P: He was a great storyteller.

G: Absolutely. And if you want to ask for it at your local bookshop, it's called 'Groucho and Me'.

P: Thanks, Mark. Great recommendations, as always.

1c

How to talk about a book 5 mins
- Give students time to read the list of phrases and tell them they are to use some of them in the next exercise.

1d

Now you: A book from your childhood 5 mins
- You may need to jog memories in some groups: *Hanni and Nanni, Struwwelpeter, Pippi Langstrumpf, Max und Moritz, Pu der Bär, Oh wie schön in Panama, Tim und Struppi, Mickey Maus, Asterix, Karl May, Die drei Musketiere, …*

2

Vocabulary: Communication technology 5+ mins
- Read out the instructions and the list before students do the pairwork activity.

3 Text   **What did you find out?**   15 mins
- Ask the class to read the first paragraph to themselves. Then ask questions 1 and 2.
- Students read the second paragraph. Ask question 3.
- Students read paragraph four. Ask question 4.
- Students read the last paragraph. Ask question 5.

Possible answers:

1 Fathers in prison can keep in touch with their children at home.

2 It's possible to produce DVDs so families can see and hear their loved ones.

3 Teachers tell the speaker to imagine that they are talking to their child. Or they can read the stories to a puppet. Volunteers read out each line and the prisoners copy them.

4 Families benefit because they don't lose contact. Fathers can be part of the family routine at home, and their children won't forget them. Prisoners learn useful new skills that could help them to get a job when they come out of prison.

5 Storybook Mums (women prisoners) and Storybook Soldiers (servicemen and women who are overseas) can record stories and messages for their children at home.

4a   **Look again**   5 mins

Possible answers: 1 Look into the camera, please. 2 Come along to Storybook Dads. 3 I don't want you to lose contact with our daughter.

4b   **Grammar: Reported speech (orders and requests)**   5 mins
- Read out the positive sentences in the Grammar box and ask volunteers to read out the negative sentences.

! If you want to spend longer on this point, look at the Language study explanation and exercises on page 106.

Extra

> **Reported speech (orders and requests)**   5 mins
> - Ask students to make the negative sentence, e.g.
>   Prompt: *He told me to sit down*.
>   Student: He told me not to sit down.
>   *He told me to tell the teacher*. (He told me not to tell …)
>   *She asked her to open the window*. (She asked her not to open …)
>   *They wanted me to go early*. (They didn't want me to go …)
>   *I asked them to phone Peter*. (I asked them not to phone …)
>   *She wanted him to help her*. (She didn't want him to help …)
>   *We told him to read it*. (We told him not to read …?)

4c   **Find some more**   5+ mins

1 The teacher told me to imagine that I was talking to Kayla. – Imagine that you are talking to Kayla.

2 She asked me to try reading the story to a puppet. – Try reading the story to a puppet. 3 My partner asked me to record the next book in a series we're reading together. – Please record the next book in the series.

4d   **A prison visit**   5+ mins

He told her … 1 to open her handbag. 2 … to take a seat in the waiting room. 3 … to follow him to the visiting area. 4 … to leave her coat by the door. 5 … not to talk to any of the other prisoners. 6 … not to try to give any money or banned items to a prisoner.

4e   **Ryan's request**   5+ mins

1 Ryan asked / wanted his partner to tell him the news from home. 2 Ryan asked / wanted his partner to kiss little Kayla for him. 3 Ryan asked / wanted his partner to wait for him. 4 Ryan didn't want his partner to forget him. / Ryan asked his partner not to forget him. 5 Ryan didn't want his partner to go off with another man. / Ryan asked his partner not to go off with another man. 6 Ryan asked / wanted his partner to send him a food parcel.

If short   - Do *Exercise 4f* as a brief class activity.
of time   - In class, have volunteers complete the first sentence and add a second sentence about learning to read.

4f   **Now you: What did they want you to do?**   5+ mins
- Follow coursebook instructions.

5   **What do you think?**   5 mins
- Students work in groups of 3 or 4 and complete the phrases and discuss the topics.

Unit 5 Step 3 Read all about it

Contents

Text topic   Newspaper sections
Functions   Talking about news media
Vocabulary   Sections of a newspaper; Prefixes
Grammar   Focus on: *by / until*
Reading   Online or on paper?

Lesson notes

www   Extra activity: www.klett-langenscheidt.de/networknow/activities (Unit 5: Step 3)

Starter   5 mins • Ask individuals to tell the class about a news story that they have heard or read recently.

1   **Close-up: Newspaper sections**   5 mins
🔑   1 Culture, 2 UK news, 3 Business, 4 Fashion, 5 Technology, 6 International

               Tip: Realia (5) Not only printed materials constitute realia. Give students a couple of easy Internet links where
               they can read or listen to English, e.g. items on *You Tube* or *Videojug*. There are several sites where the news
               is written or read in easy English, for example: http://www.newsinlevels.com

2a   **Focus on ...** *by / until*   5 mins
               • Read out the sentences and explanation in the box.

Extra
               | *by / until*   5– mins |
               | • Ask students to complete the two sentences and have individuals read them out to the class. |
               | Board: I'm going to learn English until ... |
               | I hope I'll be able to speak fluent English by ... |

2b   **Now you: Your time**   5+ mins
🔑   Possible answers: 1 I'll be at my English lesson until / till 8 pm. 2 I'll be back home after my English lesson
               by half past eight. 3 My English course will last until / till the summer holidays. 4 I have to arrive at work by
               9 am. 5 My working day lasts until / till 5 pm. 6 I always get home from work by 6 pm.

3a   **A recent survey**   10+ mins
🔑   Most Americans (66%) get their news by reading a printed newspapers.

3b   **Reading**   10 mins
               • Encourage the groups to help each other with anything that's not clear in their part of the article.

4a   **What can you remember?**   10 mins
               • Board: *   Look back at the text.
                          **   As in coursebook.
                          ***   Work on your own, without a partner.
🔑   Possible answers:
               <u>Online news:</u> The best place to find out the news is via laptops, smart phones or tablet PCs. It keeps you
               fully informed any time, any place and it's simple to update quickly. In the archive you can find articles
               from the past. Online reporting is more democratic – anyone can add to the news and they're often
               directly involved in the event. Online news is free.
               <u>Own arguments:</u> I can discuss online news with my teenage children as they read it as well. I can keep
               informed about things going on at home when I'm on holiday.

               <u>Printed news:</u> Some countries don't have the latest electronic devices and good Internet access, so they
               need printed news. More reliable – professional journalists do a lot of research and editors check the
               information is accurate. Most news stories don't change very quickly so fast updates aren't important.
               Free online news can only exist if we have printed news.
               <u>Own arguments:</u> I collect interesting articles which I cut out from the newspaper.

If short of time	• Do *Exercise 4b* as a class activity. • Do *Exercise 6* as a class activity.
4b	**Discussion** 10 mins • Follow coursebook instructions.

5a

Vocabulary building: Prefixes 5+ mins
1 rewrite, 2 anti-technology
1b), 2c), 3d), 4e), 5a)

5b
News reports 5 mins
1 ex-editor, 2 anti-war, 3 non-experts, 4 reprint, 5 misread

6
In the news 10 mins
Possible answers:
Partner A's definitions: 1 He / She goes to interview people involved in a news event. 2 He / She takes the pictures for newspapers or magazines. 3 He / She reads the news on the radio or TV. 4 He / She writes the newspaper articles. 5 He / She makes the films for news reports. 6 He / She checks if all the information and language in the news is accurate.
Partner B's definitions: 1 It's the thing you have in front of you. 2 You always get forecasts of this on the news. 3 A longer word for *ad*. 4 Pictures, sometimes with little texts that are funny. 5 A piece of informative text that you can read in the newspaper.

7
What do you think? 5+ mins
• Class discussion prompted by the quotation. If necessary, ask follow-up questions, e.g. *Which are the quality newspapers in your area? Which ones are less reliable in their reporting?*

Unit 5 Now I can

Contents Review of vocabulary, functions and structures in Unit 5

Lesson notes

www
You can download and copy a **Project sheet** to be used for the writing activities in *Now I can*: www.klett-langenscheidt.de/networknow/activities (Unit 5: Now I can)

Now I can: ... 5 mins • Ask students to look at *Now I can: ...* at the top of page 112. Remind them that the symbols refer to different skills or vocabulary items they learnt in Unit 5 and were listed in the unit aims on p. 97.

Starter Talking about communication technology; Talking about news media 10– mins

Look back ! If you have downloaded and copied the Project sheet, you can use it for this activity and for *Exercise 2b* and 4.
Possible answers: 1 The girl is listening to a story her dad, who is on prison, has recorded. The girl loves the bedtime stories. 2 The woman is reading online news. She prefers the free very latest news updates to reading the newspaper – and it's free. 3 The man is reading a newspaper. He thinks that you can only trust printed news because journalists research and check the facts.

Now look forward • Make sure that students understand *partially-sighted*. (Or: Ask if anyone knows a blind or partially-sighted person.)

Part 1 Talking about books; Talking about communication technology; Talking about news media

1 **What interests you?** 15– mins
• Have individual students ask you the questions – your answers can provide a pattern.

Part 2 Reporting what people said to you

2a What did they say? 10 mins

3/18

1 ... working ~~alone~~ in a team. 2 ... is a lifeline for many ~~younger~~ older people. 3 ... the best way to get ~~international~~ local news. 4 ... listen to the ~~headlines~~ sports report first.

1 Tanya said that she really enjoyed working in a team. 2 Richard said that the service was a lifeline for many older people. 3 Simon said that the talking newspaper was the best way to get local news. 4 Lynette said she always listened to the sports report first.

---

1 Tanya
The local paper comes out on Wednesday, so I sit down with the paper and I read it from start to finish. I choose the reports that I think are most interesting for most people. I try to include a mix of news, politics, sports, readers' letters – a bit of everything, really. I often ask for advice from colleagues. Then on Thursday, our readers come in and we record the items in our little studio. I like Thursdays. I really enjoy working in a team.

2 Richard
I think we give a good service. Yes, there are many new ways to get information and, yes, a talking newspaper is old-fashioned technology – someone sits in a studio and reads from a printed newspaper into a microphone. But it's about much more than local news. Not all of our clients are comfortable with very modern forms of technology, so we offer them the option to have the news on a CD or memory stick and a volunteer takes it to the client's

house. The service is a lifeline for many older people.

3 Simon
I get my talking newspaper on Friday. It arrives electronically. I usually listen to it at the weekend, when I have more time. During the week, I listen to a lot of radio and I get a lot of news from the television or online – I use software that reads electronic text out loud. So it's easy to get national and international news, but the talking newspaper is the best way to get local news.

4 Lynette
In our house, we're all football mad. We're big fans of our local team and my husband and I take our sons to all the home matches. Our team's too small for the television or the radio. So when my talking newspaper arrives, I'm not so interested in local politics or business – I always listen to the sports report first.

2b What else did they say? 10– mins
- You can use the Project sheet for this exercise.

Possible answers: **Tanya said that she chose the reports that she thought were most interesting for most people. Richard said that he thought they gave a good service. Simon said that he got his talking newspaper on Friday. Lynette said that in their house, they were all football mad.**

Part 3 Deal with problems when travelling

Travel problems 10 mins
- Follow coursebook intsructions.

If short of time
- Do *Exercise 4* as a class activity, with volunteers reading out their notes.

Part 4 Talking about books
Could you recommend an audiobook? 10 mins
- You can use the Project sheet for this exercise.

5 Now you choose 10+ mins
- Remind students about the star system and tell them they can choose one of the tasks.
- Students find people who want to do the same task and they work together.

And finally 5 mins • Look back at the *In this unit, you will learn to: ...* (p. 97) to show your students how much they have learnt and say how well they've done.

- Remind students about the homework pages for this lesson – the *Test yourself* pages (pp. 114/115).
- If you don't plan to use the extra pages (*English worldwide*, *English at work* and *Story*) in the lesson, students can enjoy these pages at home.

Unit 6 Step 1 Lost

Contents

Text topic	A newspaper article
Functions	Saying what went wrong; Understanding traffic reports
Vocabulary	On the road
Grammar	**You already know:** *should, could*
	And now: *should(n't) have done, could(n't) have done*

Lesson notes

www **Extra activity:** www.klett-langenscheidt.de/networknow/activities (Unit 6: Step 1)

Starter 5+ mins • Ask individual students the *Starter* question.
Possible answers: **It's very hot. There's a lot of red sand. There aren't many people. There isn't much traffic on the long roads. There are kangaroos. In the centre there's Uluru / Ayers Rock. Some Australian Aboriginals live there.**

1a **What should you do?** 5+ mins
Possible answers: **You should take a lot of water with you. Your car's tank should be full. You should take a lot of sun cream with you. You should wear a sun hat. You should have your mobile phone with you. You should tell people where you're going.**

1b **Grammar: You already know –** *should, could* 5+ mins
• Focus attention on the Grammar box and read out the sentences.

1c **You should …** 5– mins
Possible answer: **You should use sun cream, otherwise you could get sunburnt.**

Text **Tourist rescued after three days in the outback** 10+ mins
• Ask students to read the headline and look at the photos and the caption. Then ask volunteers to speculate what the story is about – but don't give any indication as to whether the speculations are correct or not, just answer: *Could be / Maybe*, etc.
• Students then read the article to themselves.

2 **So many mistakes!** 5+ mins
He set off alone. He didn't have enough water with him. The battery of his mobile phone was low. He wore the wrong clothes – a black T-shirt, sandals and no hat. He had no sun cream.

3a **Grammar: And now –** *should(n't) have, could(n't) have* 5+ mins
• Focus attention on the Grammar box and read out the sentences.
• Ask: *Are these sentences about the past or present?* (past)
! For more explanations and practice, you can look at the Language study on page 123.

Extra
> *should(n't)* 5+ mins
> • Ask students to tell you what you should(n't) have done. Read out the prompts:
> *I was late for work this morning …*
> *I went to a party and drank too much.* (You shouldn't have drunk so much.)
> *I left the party very late.* (You should have left earlier / shouldn't have left so late.)
> *I waited for the last bus home and I didn't take a taxi.* (You should have taken a taxi.)
> *I went to bed late.* (You should have gone to bed earlier / shouldn't have gone to bed so late.)
> *I forgot to set my alarm clock.* (You should have set / shouldn't have forgotten to set the alarm.)
> *I overslept.* (You shouldn't have overslept.)
> *I didn't apologise to my boss.* (You should have apologised.)

6 Location | Step 1 | Lost

3b What should he have done? 5 mins
2 black – He should have chosen a white T-shirt. 3 hat – He should have protected his head with a hat.
4 the right shoes – He should have worn the right shoes on his feet. 5 water – He should have taken a lot of water in his bottle. 6 guide – He should have asked a guide to go with him.

3c What could he have done? 5+ mins
Possible answers: I think he could have shouted for help. He probably couldn't have made an SOS signal. I think he could have made shade (with his T-shirt). He probably couldn't have found water. I think he could have tried to walk at night, not during the day.

If short of time
• *Exercise 3d* can be printed out and set as a homework task – see **www** on page 47.

3d What happened next? 5+ mins
• Read out the instructions and play ▶ 3/25.

3/25

He did the same thing again and waited until he was in serious trouble before raising the alarm that he was lost.

(M = man, W = woman)
W: Is there something funny in the newspaper?
M: Do you remember last week there was that story in the news about the British tourist who got lost in the Australian outback?
W: Oh yes, the man who was lost for days and he didn't even have a sunhat with him. He was red from head to toe when they found him.
M: That's the one. Well, he's done it again!
W: He's got lost again?
M: Yes. Listen to this: A British tourist was rescued from the Australian outback yesterday – for the second time in less than a week. Martin Lake, 50, was found by a police helicopter after he had walked around less than a mile from the area where he was first lost near Alice Springs in Central Australia. This time he was lost for four days – one day longer than the first time.
W: That's unbelievable. What was he thinking? Did he remember his sunhat and some factor 50 sun cream this time, at least?
M: It doesn't say. It says: Although his phone was in better working order the second time, he waited until he was in serious trouble before raising the alarm that he was lost.
W: Yes, he was probably too embarrassed to call earlier.
M: Local people, concerned that Mr Lake might put his own life – and that of rescuers – in danger again, joined in a united chorus: "Send him home!"
W: As long as he can find his way to the airport without getting lost again …

3e Now you choose: What did you do wrong? 5+ mins
• Students choose which task they'd like to do and work in small groups. It doesn't matter if they have chosen different tasks.

4a Vocabulary: On the road 5+ mins
3a), 4b), 5c), 2d), 6e), 7f), 8g), 1h)

4b How to understand a traffic report 5+ mins
• Read out the phrases.

4c Problems on the roads 10 mins
• Read out the first part of the instructions and play ▶ 3/26.
3/26–27
• Read out the second part of the instructions and play ▶ 3/27.

Union Street in the city centre – closed until Friday because of roadworks.
Milton Park roundabout on the A34 – traffic lights are out of order.

Drivers should follow the diversion signs and allow extra time for their journey.
Drivers should drive carefully as they approach the roundabout.

Local radio traffic report presenter:

It's busy on the roads this morning, but traffic is generally flowing well, with no reports of long delays. The M4 motorway is clear in both directions.

The first thing I need to warn you about this morning is Union Street in the city centre, where the roadworks are still in place. Union Street has been closed since Monday because of these roadworks, and will remain closed until Friday. Diversions are in place. So, follow the diversion signs and allow a little extra time for your journey if you're in that part of town. Police say the diversion is working well.

And the only other problem this morning is on the A34. It's the Milton Park roundabout on the A34, where the traffic lights are out of order. The police tell us that the lights should be repaired soon, but in the meantime, drivers are advised to drive carefully as they approach the Milton Park roundabout on the A34. Apart from those two items, there are no incidents in the area this morning and traffic is moving well. So I'll hand you back to the studio.

5 **What do you think?** 5 mins
- In class, students give their opinions on the pictures. Encourage discussion by asking follow-up questions: *How often do you use your car? What was the worst traffic jam you were in?*

Unit 6 Step 2 Retiring abroad

Contents

Text topic A magazine article about retiring abroad
Functions Explaining advantages and disadvantages; Talking about live in different parts of the world
Vocabulary Different aspects of a country
Grammar **You already know:** The gerund *(-ing)* (1) after certain verbs
 And now: The gerund *(-ing)* (2) as a subject and after prepositions

Lesson notes

www **Extra activity:** www.klett-langenscheidt.de/networknow/activities (Unit 6: Step 2)

Starter 5 mins • Ask individual students the *Starter* question.

Text **Retire to the sun!** 10 mins
- Read out the introductory paragraph and ask students where they would like to retire to – either within their own country or abroad.
- Ask students to read the article to themselves and tick the places that mention a good climate. (S.W. France + Florida)
- Ask how important a good climate is to them and why.

1a **Vocabulary: Aspects of life in different countries** 5+ mins
🔑 1c), 2i), 3a), 4d), 5h), 6g), 7e), 8b), 9f)

1b **Now you: Where would you like to go?** 5+ mins
- Follow coursebook instructions.

1c **How to talk about advantages and disadvantages** 5– mins
- Give students time to read the list of phrases and tell them they are to use some of them in the next exercise.

1d **Moving abroad** 5 mins
- Follow coursebook instructions.

2a   **Grammar: You already know – The gerund *(-ing)* (1) after certain verbs**   5 mins
- Read out the sentences in the Grammar box and remind students that we use the gerund to talk about activities we *like, love, dislike, enjoy, hate* doing.

! If you want to spend longer on this point, look at the Language study explanation and exercises on page 128.

2b   **Now you: Would you enjoy living in Antigua?**   5 mins
- Follow coursebook instructions.

3a   **Grammar: And now – The gerund *(-ing)* (2) as a subject and after prepositions**   5 mins
- Read the first section – the gerund as a subject, i.e. at the beginning of a sentence.
- Read out the second section – the gerund after prepositions, e.g. *at, for, in, about, by, of.*

! If you want to spend longer on this point, look at the Language study explanation and exercises on page 128.

Extra
> **Gerund (1) / (2)**   5 mins
> - Ask students to use a gerund to complete sentences about themselves and then read them out to the class.
>   Board:
>   I really enjoy _____
>   I've never liked _____
>   _____ is my favourite pastime.
>   I'm happy about _____

3b   **Another way to say it**   5 mins
1 Moving here is the ideal option if you want a quiet life in the countryside.
2 Getting the relevant immigration papers isn't easy(, but it's worth it).
3 Employing a housekeeper is a realistic option.

All these sentences have a gerund as the subject.

3c   **Now you: What are you looking forward to?**   5 mins
- Accept answers with a noun or a gerund, e.g. *I'm looking forward to my holidays / going on holiday.*

4a   **Problems in paradise**   10+ mins
- Read out the first part of the instructions and play ▶ 3/33.
- ↓ Divide the class into two groups: Ask Students A to make notes about the positive aspects and Students B to make notes about the problematic aspects.
- Read out the second part of the instructions and play ▶ 3/34.
  positive: cheap house prices and cost of living, sun all the year round, a relaxed lifestyle, good medical care
  problematic aspects: driving on the other side of the road, using public transport, organising help at home, communicating with doctors, falling exchange rates, loss of money when they sold their villa
  ✓ **2, 4, 6**
  Corrected sentences: **1 Paul only needed a routine operation. 3 They could speak basic Spanish.**
  5 Exchange rates started to fall.

> (RP = radio presenter, PW = Paul Wallis, SW = Sally Wallis)
> RP: In today's Money Report, we're looking at the trend for retiring abroad. Retiring abroad can seem a very attractive option for many people for many reasons. House prices and the cost of living are often cheaper in other countries than at home. There's the attraction of sun all the year round and a relaxed lifestyle. Spain, in particular, has been a popular destination for many years and is currently home to more than 50,000 UK pensioners. But it's not all 'fun in the sun'.
> When they retired, Yorkshire couple Paul and Sally Wallis bought a three-bedroom villa on the Costa Blanca with sea views and a pool. For two years they enjoyed the holiday lifestyle in their Spanish paradise – playing golf, walking on the beach and eating out in local restaurants two or three nights a week. But after those two years, they decided to come home again. So, what happened? Paul and Sally are with me today. Hello Paul, Sally.

PW & SW:	Hello.
RP:	So, Paul, when did things start to go wrong?
PW:	Well, the first problem was that I had to stop driving because of a medical problem.
SW:	I can drive, but I'd never driven in Spain because I didn't like driving on the other side of the road. I didn't feel confident.
PW:	Yes, so, anyway, while I was waiting for my operation, life became more difficult because we had to use public transport for shopping, doctor's appointments, etc. And the nearest bus stop was about half a kilometre from our villa.
SW:	Luckily, Paul only needed a routine operation and he was able to have it under the Spanish national health system and he got better quite quickly, but it made us think about the future. What would we do if Paul could never drive again, or if one of us was seriously ill?
RP:	But the medical care was good?
PW:	Oh, yes. As a European citizen, you get the same care as a Spanish person. That was one of the main reasons why we chose a country in the European Union, so medical care wouldn't be a problem.
SW:	But we had no idea how to organise help for Paul at home after his operation. The system was, well, foreign.
RP:	And was the language a problem?
SW:	Yes, definitely. We'd spent most of our time in the ex-pat community, with all the other British people. We knew basic Spanish for shopping and restaurants and that sort of thing …
PW:	But it was difficult to communicate with doctors about my medical problem. They spoke good English, but somehow it's not the same.
SW:	When you're ill, you want to know exactly what's going on, don't you?
RP:	And I think there were financial problems too?
PW:	Yes. Our pensions are British, of course, and so they were paid into our British bank account in pounds and we transferred them into our Spanish account in Euros. At first that was fine, but then exchange rates started to fall and when we changed the money into Euros, the amount started getting smaller from one month to the next.
RP:	So, in the end, you decided to move back.
SW:	Yes. We sold the villa – for less money than we'd paid for it – and came home.
PW:	I believe we got out at the right time. When we saw what happened to the Spanish economy after we left, I think we were lucky.
RP:	So, after your experience, what advice would you give to other people who might be thinking of retiring abroad?
PW:	I think the first thing people need to think about is …

If short of time
- Do *Exercise 4b* as a brief class activity.
- In class, have volunteers complete only the second sentence in *Exercise 5*: *The best thing about retirement is …*

4b **What advice would you give?** 10 mins
Possible answers: **Think about what would happen if you got ill. Get a good health insurance. Learn the language of the country you move to. Keep in contact with your friends at home. Make sure there's good public transport.**

5 **What do you think?** 5 mins
- Students work in groups of 3 or 4 and complete the phrases and discuss the topics.

Unit 6 Step 3 Searching online

Contents

Text topic Computer instructions
Functions Understanding computer instructions
Vocabulary Computer instructions; Verbs with prepositions
Grammar Focus on: *so … (that) / such a(n) … (that)*
Reading A real *home*page

Lesson notes

www **Extra activity:** www.klett-langenscheidt.de/networknow/activities (Unit 6: Step 3)

Starter 5 mins • Ask individual students the *Starter* questions.

1a **Close-up: Installation instructions** 5 mins
1 insert, 2 double-click, 3 icon, 4 enter, 5 (user) password, 6 screen

Tip: Realia (6) When you buy a new appliance, e.g. kitchen machines or computer equipment, there are often instructions in English – copy these and save them. You can make your own gap-fill activity or have a student read the instructions out and the class guess what the appliance is. It's worth investing a bit of time to file the items under topic headings so that you can access them easily for future use.

1b **Using a computer** 10 mins
2a), 6b), 8c), 3d), 7e), 1f), 4g), 5h)

2 **Now you: Finding your way** 5+ mins
• Follow coursebook instructions.

3 **Reading** 15 mins
• Students read the five paragraphs of the article to themselves.
• Then they decide if the five statements on the board are true or false and correct the false statements.
Board:

1 Guddu went to sleep on the train.	(No – Saroo went to sleep.)
2 An American couple adopted Saroo.	(No – an Australian couple adopted him.)
3 Saroo used Google Earth to find his old home.	(True.)
4 Saroo's mother hadn't seen him for 25 years.	(True.)
5 Saroo now lives in Khandwa.	(No – he lives in Tasmania.)

• Students then remember what the six numbers refer to.
• ↓ Students can refer to the text.
Saroo was <u>five</u> when he got lost. He got off a train at a station about <u>two</u> hours from home. He slept for <u>twelve</u> hours. When he was <u>30</u>, he discovered Google Earth. The Calcutta train could have travelled about <u>1,000</u> kilometres. Saroo had been lost for <u>25</u> years.

4 **What can you remember?** 10 mins
• Board:

*	Underline the information in the text and read it out.
**	As in coursebook.
***	Add sentences about the location *train*.

Saroo fell asleep on the <u>platform</u>. He was in <u>Calcutta</u> when he woke up. Someone from a <u>children's home</u> found Saroo and looked after him. An Australian couple adopted him and took him to <u>Tasmania</u>. <u>Khandwa</u> is Saroo's village. His mother had moved from their old <u>house</u>.

If short of time
• Do *Exercise 5* as a class activity.
• Do *Exercise 6d* as a class activity.

5 **Vocabulary building: Verbs with prepositions** 5+ mins
1 off, 2 on, 3 up, 4 after, 5 for, 6 out

6a   **Focus on ...** *so ... (that) / such a(n) ... (that)*   5+ mins
- Read out the sentences and explanation in the box.

Extra

> *so ... (that) / such a(n) ... that*   5+ mins
> - Ask students to rephrase your sentences, beginning with *It* and using *such*:
>   *The book was so interesting that I want to read it again.* (It was such an interesting book ...)
>   *The exam was so difficult that I couldn't do it.* (It was such a difficult exam ...)
>   *The computer was so expensive that I didn't buy it.* (It was such an expensive computer ...)
>   *The weather was so bad that we couldn't go out.* (It was such bad weather ...)
>   *The pudding was so sweet that I couldn't eat it.* (It was such a sweet pudding ...)
>   *The film was so boring that I fell asleep.* (It was such a boring film ...)

6b   **Such an incredible story**   5+ mins
1 ~~so~~ | such, 2 so | ~~such~~, 3 so | ~~such~~, 4 ~~so~~ | such 5 so | ~~such~~

6c   **It was so amazing that he found his home**   5+ mins
1 Saroo's family were so poor that their children had to work. 2 India is such a big country that it's difficult to find one small village. 3 Saroo was so young when he got lost that he didn't know the name of his village. 4 Google Earth has such an exact search function that you can find anywhere in the world.

6d   **Now you: Your opinion**   10– mins
- Follow coursebook instructions.

7   **What do you think?**   5+ mins
- Class discussion prompted by the quotation. If necessary, ask follow-up questions, e.g. *How much time do you spend at your computer? What activities has your computer replaced?* (e.g. writing letters).

Unit 6 Now I can

Contents   Review of vocabulary, functions and structures in Unit 6

Lesson notes

www   You can download and copy a **Project sheet** to be used for the writing activities in *Now I can*: www.klett-langenscheidt.de/networknow/activities (Unit 6: Now I can)

Now I can: ...   5 mins   • Ask students to look at *Now I can: ...* at the top of page 134. Remind them that the symbols refer to different skills or vocabulary items they learnt in Unit 6 and were listed in the unit aims on p. 119.

Starter   **Saying what went wrong; Talking about life in different parts of the world**   10– mins

Look back
Possible answers:
Martin Lake got lost in the Australian outback – twice.
Paul and Sally Wallis retired to Spain but came back home again.
Saroo fell asleep on a train near his home in India. It took him to Calcutta. He was adopted and he grew up in Tasmania but he found his home again after 25 years.

Now look forward   • Ask students if they have been to South Africa.

6 Location | Now I can

Part 1   Explaining advantages and disadvantages; Talking about life in different parts of the world

1a   **What do you know?**   10– mins
- Have students work in groups and pool their ideas, which can then be shared in class.
  Possible answers:
  3 capital cities: Pretoria, Cape Town, Bloemfontein.
  Johannesburg: largest city, high crime rate.
  11 official languages, including English and Afrikaans (from Dutch settlers).
  The *Springboks* are the national rugby team.
  Currency: Rand.
  Soweto (<u>So</u>uth <u>We</u>stern <u>To</u>wnships): township of apartheid protest pre-1990.
  Tourist attractions: Table Mountain, Kruger National Park.
  Nelson Mandela: anti-apartheid activist and politician (S.A. president 1994–1999), imprisoned for 27 years on Robben Island.

1b   **What's life like there?**   10– mins
  ! If you have downloaded and copied the Project sheet, you can use it for this exercise, *Exercise 2c* and *Part 3*.
  Possible answers: **The climate is better. It's more dangerous – depending where you live. The countryside is more varied and has more interesting animal life.**

Part 2   Saying what went wrong; Understanding traffic reports

2a   **Driving in South Africa**   5+ mins
  In Germany, there are speed limits on secondary roads, not on motorways; seat belts are compulsory; drinking and driving is prohibited, too.

2b   **What went wrong?**   10 mins
  ⊙ 3/43
- ↓ Students choose a heading for each of the seven texts before listening again and doing the coursebook task.
  Board:

Wear your seatbelt!	(6)
Don't drink and drive!	(1)
No self-service!	(4)
No speeding!	(7)
Beware of thieves!	(2)
Don't feed the animals!	(3)
Pay for services!	(5)

- Play ▶ 3/43 and stop the CD after each of the seven speakers.
  1 She drank too much and drove back to the hotel. – She should have taken a taxi.
  2 He drove with open windows and someone stole his bag from the car at the red traffic lights. –
  He should have closed the windows while he was waiting at the traffic lights.
  3 She fed a wild monkey by the side of the road and was bitten. – She shouldn't have stopped to feed the monkey.
  4 He filled his car at the petrol station himself. – He should have waited for the attendant to fill it.
  5 He just said thank you to the boy at the petrol station who cleaned his windscreen. – He should have given the boy some money.
  6 He drove without his seatbelt on. – He should have put his seatbelt on.
  7 She drove at 140 on a highway. – She should have thought about the speed limit.

  ---

  1 I was really stupid. It was late in the evening, I drank three beers and then I drove back to the hotel. Stupid, I know. And of course, the police stopped me.
  2 It was really hot, so I drove with the windows open. That was a mistake because that part of town has a very high crime rate. While I was waiting at the traffic lights, someone reached into the car and stole my bag.
  3 We were on a little road in a rural area and we saw a really sweet monkey by the side of the road, so we stopped and gave it some food. Then it wanted more food and we didn't have any – and it bit me!
  4 The first time we went to a petrol station, I got out of the car and started filling the car. I didn't know the system. The attendant came out and started shouting at me.
  5 The boy at the petrol station cleaned my windscreen, so I smiled and said thank you, but he knocked on my car window and held out his hand. Then of course I understood what he wanted.

6 A policeman stopped me and that's when I realised that I'd forgotten to put my seatbelt on. It was a stupid mistake – and an expensive one! It was quite a large fine.

7 In Germany we don't have a speed limit on the Autobahn, that's our motorway or highway, so I didn't really think about the speed limit when I was driving on the big highways in South Africa. I drove a bit too fast – only about 140 – and I got a fine from the South African police.

2c

A traffic report   10 mins

- You can use the Project sheet for this exercise.
- Play ▶ 3/44. Students listen and note down the three problems.

Problem 1: There's a fire near the N2. The road is still open in both directions, but there's a lot of smoke about. People should drive slowly and carefully and expect delays.

Problem 2: The traffic lights on Ocean Way in the Sunset Beach area are out of order. People must take care if they're driving to Sunset Beach.

Problem 3: The R44 highway is closed in both directions outside Wellington because of farm protests. The police are diverting traffic through the town centre. People must follow the diversion signs and should allow extra time for their journey.

Local radio reporter:

Welcome back. You're listening to Western Cape Radio and I have a traffic report for you if you're on the roads around Cape Town this afternoon.

First, there's a problem on the N2. That's the N2 in both directions – coming into the city and also leaving the city. There's a fire near the road. It isn't on the road itself, so the road is still open, but there's a lot of smoke about, so please drive slowly and extra carefully on the N2 this afternoon and expect delays.

Next, we're in the Sunset Beach area. We have a report of traffic lights out of order on Ocean Way. That's traffic lights on Ocean Way, not working. So take care there if you're driving to Sunset Beach today.

And last today we're going out of town to Wellington on the R44 highway. The R44 highway is closed outside Wellington. That's due to the farm protests there today. The highway is closed in both directions and the police are diverting through the town centre. So follow the diversion signs and allow extra time for your journey.

That's all for now. More later.

If short of time
- Do *Part 3* as a class activity, with volunteers completing the sentences.

Part 3

Explaining advantages and disadvantages; Understanding computer instructions

What's best?   10 mins
- You can use the Project sheet for this exercise.

4

Now you choose   10 mins
- Remind students about the star system and tell them they can choose one of the tasks.
- Students find a partner who wants to do the same task and they work together.

And finally   5 mins   • Look back at the *In this unit, you will learn to: ...* (p. 119) to show your students how much they have learnt in this unit and say how well they've done.
- Remind students about the homework pages for this lesson – the *Test yourself* pages (pp. 136/137).
- If you don't plan to use the extra pages (*English worldwide* and *English at work*) in the lesson, students can enjoy these pages at home.

English worldwide, English at work, Story / Playing with English

Lesson notes for the optional pages *English worldwide, English at work, Story / Playing with English* after each unit

One unit consists of three steps and the *Now I can* review lesson. The six units provide a total of 24 lessons. Each of the three optional pages after every unit is designed to provide teaching material for approximately 30 minutes, so you can use all of the pages to fill a 90-minute lesson. Or you can use individual pages as 'fillers' if your lesson is longer than 90 minutes.

1 English worldwide
- After every unit, there's a page which focusses on a different English-speaking country.
- There's a text related to the unit theme. It has a glossary so that students can easily read the text at home if you decide not to use it in class.
- There's a key at the back of the coursebook so students can do the exercises at home.
- The *Listen in* exercise gives the student the opportunity to hear a native of the country speaking freely about an aspect of the text. This is unscripted, authentic speech.
- The exercise *They say it differently* points out a linguistic difference particular to that country.
- Finally, *Find out …* is an Internet task to encourage students to use English in 'real life'.

2 English at work
- The second optional page is one related to using English in the workplace.
- Each of the six pages deals with one typical work situation.
- There's a phrase box to provide students with the vocabulary to deal with the situation. The phrases are recorded so that students can practise them at home if you decide not to use this page in class. There's a key at the back of the coursebook so students can do the exercises at home.
- The exercise *They say / do it differently* points out a linguistic or cultural difference in English-speaking workplaces.

3 Story
- After Units 1, 3 and 5, there's a story – reading for pleasure.
- It's a story related to the unit theme. It has a glossary so that students can easily read the text at home if you decide not to use it in class.

or

3 Playing with English
- After Units 2, 4 and 6, there's a game which practises structures and vocabulary from the previous unit.

If you decide to use the optional pages as classroom material, here are some teaching notes for them.

Unit 1 English worldwide
(coursebook p. 28)

Living in Manhattan – A text about accommodation in New York.

NB You can find the keys to the exercises on page 145 of the coursebook. You can find the audio scripts on page 151.

Starter 5– mins
- Brainstorm *accommodation* by asking: *What are the most expensive cities to rent a flat in your country?*

Text: Living in Manhattan 🎧1/20   10+ mins
- Before playing CD 1/20, tell students they're going to listen to a text about living in Manhattan. Ask: *Why does the population of Manhattan double on weekdays?* (Because commuters travel into the city for work.)
- Students then read the text to check their answers.
- With books closed, students say what they can remember about the following numbers:
  Board: 59km² 1.6 million 3.9 million $4,000 35 to 50
- Pairwork: Discussion on the task in the box.

They say it differently   5 mins

Radio quiz: New York 🎧1/21   5 mins

Listen in 🎧1/22   5 mins
NB The transcript for *Listen in* can be found online: www.klett-langenscheidt.de/networknow/audioscripts
- Tell the students that this is a recording of an American woman chatting to someone in the recording studios. It's an authentic recording. They won't understand every word the American says, but they'll be able to understand enough to do the task.

Finally …
- Point out the Internet task for the students to do at home.

Unit 1 English at work (coursebook p. 29)

Welcome to our company

NB You can find the keys to the exercises on page 145 of the coursebook. You can find the audioscripts on pages 151/152.

Starter: Visitors   5 mins

1a Phrases to welcome visitors 🎧1/23   5 mins
- After students have compared their phrases in class, play ▶ 1/23 and have them repeat the phrases.

1b Welcoming visitors ⊙1/24–25 5+ mins
- Read out the first part of the instructions and play ▶ 1/24.
- Read out the second part of the instructions. Play ▶ 1/25. Students listen again and volunteers answer.

1c What does it mean? + They say it differently 5 mins

2a Phrases to show someone round 5 mins
- Read out the phrases in the box and have students repeat them.

2b Roleplay 5 mins

Unit 1 Story (coursebook p. 30)

Neighbours
- Photocopy the *Story* page – one for each student – and cut it into these 5 sections: Saturday morning, 9am; 11am + 1pm; 4pm; 6pm; *Glossary*.

- Tell the class the title of the story: *Neighbours*. Ask: *How do you get on with your neighbours? What problems can there be between neighbours?*
- Hand out the *Glossary* and have students read through the phrases. Then ask volunteers to think of a situation in which they use one of the phrases.
- Hand out the 11am + 1pm section. Students read it and speculate what the story could be about.
- Then hand out the 4pm section. Ask for further speculation.
- Give out the Saturday morning section. Ask for speculation.
- Hand out the 6pm section and have volunteers summarise the story.
- Students open their books at page 30 and read the complete story. Point out that they can listen to the story online: www.klett-langenscheidt.de/networknow/story

Unit 2 English worldwide
(coursebook p. 50)

Made in Scotland – A text about Scottish inventions.

NB You can find the keys to the exercises on page 146 of the coursebook.

Starter 5 mins
- Brainstorm *inventions* by asking: *Which inventions of the twentieth century would you not like to be without?* – and make a list on the board.
- Take a class vote on the top five.

Text: Made in Scotland ⊙1/46 10 mins
- Before students look at the text, tell them they're going to listen to a text about Scottish inventions and they should note down as many as they can. Play ▶ 1/46.
- Students pool their ideas in class.
- Students then read the text and find any inventions they missed.
- Pairwork: Discussion on the task in the box.

They say it differently 5 mins

Listen in ⊙1/47 5 mins
NB The transcript for *Listen in* can be found online: www.klett-langenscheidt.de/networknow/audioscripts
- Tell the students that this is a recording of a Scottish person chatting to someone in the recording studios. It's an authentic recording. They won't understand every word the Scotsman says, but they'll be able to understand enough to do the task.

Info 5 mins
- Ask the class: *Why is a person from Scotland not happy if you say he is Scotch?*
- Students read the text to find the answer.

Finally …
- Point out the Internet task for the students to do at home.

Unit 2 English at work (coursebook p. 51)

Placing an order

NB You can find the keys to the exercises on page 146 of the coursebook. You can find the audio scripts on page 153.

Starter: Ordering goods 5– mins

1a Phrases to order products ⊙1/48 5 mins
- After students have compared their phrases in class, play ▶ 1/48 and have students repeat the phrases.

1b Do you offer a discount? ⊙1/49 + They do it differently 5+ mins
- Read out the instructions in *1b* and play ▶ 1/49.
- Remind students that register is important in language. For example, you would use different words and phrases when speaking to a child or to your bank manager.

1c Formal or informal? 5 mins

1d Listen again ⊙1/50 5– mins
- Read out the instructions and play ▶ 1/50.

2 Choose a task 5 mins
- Here students have the chance to practise making a phone call or writing an email.

Unit 2 Playing with English
(coursebook p. 52)

Patchwork game
- A lighthearted way to practise vocabulary and structures from the previous unit.

Unit 3 English worldwide
(coursebook p. 72)

Hurling – an ancient Irish sport – A text about one of Ireland's national sports.

NB You can find the keys to the exercises on page 147 of the coursebook.

Starter   5– mins
- Brainstorm *sport* by asking: *Which unusual sports have you heard of?*

Text: Hurling – and ancient Irish sport 🎧2/22   5+ mins
- Tell students they're going to listen to a text about an unusual sport. They should choose the correct information in the sentences on the board.
- Board: Hurling is an English / Irish sport.   (Irish)
  It's a modern / old sport.   (old)
- Play ▶ 2/22.
- Students then read the text on page 72 to check their answers.
- In class: Discussion on the task in the box.

Did you know?   5– mins
! This information may lead to your being asked about the difference between Great Britain and the United Kingdom. Great Britain consists of England, Scotland and Wales. The full name of the United Kingdom is the United Kingdom of Great Britain and Northern Ireland, so the UK consists of England, Scotland, Wales and Northern Ireland.

They say it differently   5– mins
- Before reading the text, ask which bi-lingual countries students know. (Belgium, Canada, India, Wales, …)

What does it mean?   5 mins

Listen in 🎧1/23   5 mins
- **NB** The transcript for *Listen in* can be found online: www.klett-langensheidt.de/networknow/audioscripts
- Tell the students that this is a recording of an Irish girl chatting to someone in the recording studios. It's an authentic recording. They won't understand every word the Irish girl says, but they'll be able to understand enough to do the task.

Finally …
- Point out the Internet task for the students to do at home.

Unit 3 English at work (coursebook p. 73)

Presenting ideas

NB You can find the keys to the exercises on page 147 of the coursebook. You can find the audio scripts on page 155.

Starter: Presentations   5– mins

1a Phrases for presentations 🎧2/24   5– mins
- After students have compared their phrases in class, play ▶ 2/24 and have them repeat the phrases.

1b A presentation 🎧2/25–26   5+ mins
- Read out the first part of the instructions. Play ▶ 2/25.
- Play ▶ 2/26. Students answer the second question.

They do it differently   5– mins

1c I'd like us to look at this …   5 mins

2 A mini-presentation   5+ mins

Unit 3 Story (coursebook p. 74)

A protest
- Give students time to read the story to themselves – remind them that the *Glossary* is there to help them with vocabulary.
- Ask the following comprehension questions:
  What time did the store close? (At 8 o'clock.)
  Where did the woman hide? (In the toilets.)
  When did she leave her hiding place? (At midnight.)
  Which department did she go to? (The toy department.)
  What kind of dolls did she work on? (Princess dolls and soldier dolls.)
  When did she leave the building? (In the morning – like a normal customer.)
  What surprise would children get on Christmas morning when they played with their new dolls? (The princess would say: "I can kill you with my hands." The soldier would say: "I love pink lipstick.")
  What was she protesting about? (About gender-specific toys.)
- As an additional activity, students can write a summary of the story.
- Point out that students can listen to the story online: www.klett-langenscheidt.de/networknow/story

Unit 4 English worldwide
(coursebook p. 94)

Sun protection down under – A text about precautions against the Australian sun.

NB You can find the keys to the exercises on page 148 of the coursebook.

Starter   5 mins
- Read out the title: *Sun protection down under.* Ask: *Which country is this text about?* (Australia) *Why is it called 'down under'?* (Because it's on the other side of the world.)

Text: Sun protection down under 🎧2/44   10 mins
- Before students look at the text, tell them they're going to listen to a text about the Australian climate and they should listen for information so they can complete the sentences on the board.

Board:

> The highest temperature recorded in Australia was
> _____.
> Australia has the highest rate of _____ in
> the world.
> The five tips for sun protections are:
> Wear _____
> Apply _____
> Put on a _____
> Look for _____
> Put on _____

- Play ▶ 2/44.
- Students then read the text on page 94 and check their answers.
- Pairwork: Discussion on the task in the box.

They say it differently   5 mins

What does it mean?   5 mins

Listen in 🎧2/45   5 mins
NB The transcript for *Listen in* can be found online:
www.klett-langenscheidt.de/networknow/audioscripts
- Tell the students that this is a recording of an Australian chatting to someone in the recording studios. It's an authentic recording. They won't understand every word the Australian says, but they'll be able to understand enough to do the task.

Finally …
- Point out the Internet task for the students to do at home.

Unit 5 English worldwide

(coursebook p. 116)

Words from India – A text about languages in India.

NB You can find the keys to the exercises on page 149 of the coursebook.

Starter   5– mins
- Ask: *Which English words are sometimes used in German?* Tell students that words which are adopted from mother languages are called *loanwords*.

Text: Words from India 🎧3/21   10 mins
- Before playing CD 3/21, tell students they're going to listen to a text about languages in India. Ask: *Which two Indian loanwords are mentioned in the text?* (pyjamas and bungalow) Students then read the text to check their answers.
- Pairwork: Discussion on the task in the box.

They say it differently   5 mins

Loanwords quiz   5 mins

Listen in 🎧3/22   5 mins
NB The transcript for *Listen in* can be found online:
www.klett-langenscheidt.de/networknow/audioscripts

Unit 4 English at work (coursebook p. 95)

Customer complaints

NB You can find the keys to the exercises on page 148 of the coursebook. You can find the audio scripts on page 156.

Starter: Sending it back   5– mins

1a Phrases to describe faulty goods 🎧2/46   5– mins
- After students have compared their phrases in class, play ▶ 2/46 and have them repeat the phrases.

1b A call to customer services 🎧2/47   5– mins
- Read out the instructions and play ▶ 2/47.

1c Phrases to deal with customer complaints 🎧2/49 +
1d Customer services 🎧2/48   5 mins
- Play ▶ 2/49 and have students repeat the phrases in *1c*.
- Read out the instructions in *1d* and play ▶ 2/48.

1e Dealing with complaints   5– mins

They say it differently   5– mins

2a What happened?   5 mins

2b Role play   5+ mins

Unit 4 Playing with English

(coursebook p. 96)

Lucky words
- A lighthearted way to practise vocabulary from the previous unit.

- Tell the students that this is a recording of an Indian man chatting to someone in the recording studios. It's an authentic recording. They won't understand every word the Indian says, but they'll be able to understand enough to do the task.

Finally …
- Point out the Internet task for the students to do at home.

Unit 5 English at work (coursebook p. 117)

Meetings

NB You can find the keys to the exercises on page 149 of the coursebook. You can find the audioscripts on page 158.

Starter: Your meetings   5 mins

1a Phrases for chairing meetings 🎧3/23 +
1b The Monday meeting 🎧3/24   5+ mins
- After students have compared their phrases in class, play ▶ 3/23 and have them repeat the phrases in *1a*.
- Read out the instructions in *1b* and play ▶ 3/24.

1c Meeting words   5 mins

They do it differently   5 mins
- Have students use the given phrases to introduce themselves to four other people.

2 A class meeting   10+ mins
- Take part in the meeting yourself so you can discreetly add to the discussion – you can put forward teachers' request.

Unit 5 Story (coursebook p. 118)

What did she say?

- Give students time to read the story on page 118 and ask *What was the misunderstanding?* (Yvonne said *warrior*; Jenny thought she said *worrier*.)
- Tell the class you're going to summarise the story but you need their help to complete the details. They should repeat your sentence and complete it.
  Two women were waiting at … (the bus stop.) *Jenny is the vicar's wife and lives …* (next to the church.) *Yvonne has just moved to the village. Yvonne knows about Jenny from the woman in …* (the village shop.) *The woman told Yvonne that Jenny was …* (a real warrior.) *When Yvonne told Jenny that, Jenny misunderstood. She thought the woman said that she was …* (a real worrier.) *Jenny and Yvonne got on the bus and Jenny couldn't stop thinking about being a real worrier. So she asked Yvonne, "Did the woman in the shop really say …* (I was a worrier?") *Yvonne looked confused and said, "Oh no – she didn't say …* (you were a worrier, she said you were a real warrior.") *She said you were a fighter, a strong woman – someone who gets things done. She said you were like …* (that old Queen Boudicca.)
- Point out that they can listen to the story online: www.klett-langenscheidt.de/networknow/story

Unit 6 English worldwide
(coursebook p. 138)

Penguins in Africa – A text about wildlife in South Africa

NB You can find the keys to the exercises on page 149 of the coursebook.

Starter   5 mins
- Ask: *Which animals do you associate with Africa?* (elephants, antelopes, zebras, lions, etc.)

Text: Penguins in Africa 3/46   10 mins
- Before students look at the text, tell them they're going to listen to a text about the animals in South Africa and they should note down the kinds of animal mentioned. (lion, elephant, buffalo, rhinoceros, leopard, penguin)
- Play ▶ 3/46.
- Students then read the text on page 138 and check their answers.
- Class activity: answer the questions in the task in the box.

NB Penguins live only in the Southern Hemisphere – on the fringes of Antarctica (but not at the South Pole itself). Some species live in Argentina, Australia and New Zealand.

They say it differently   5 mins

Listen in 3/47   5 mins
NB The transcript for *Listen in* can be found online: www.klett-langenscheidt.de/networknow/audioscripts
- Tell the students that this is a recording of a South African woman chatting to someone in the recording studios. It's an authentic recording. They won't understand every word the South African says, but they'll be able to understand enough to do the task.

What does it mean?   5 mins

Finally …
- Point out the Internet task for the students to do at home.

Unit 6 English at work (coursebook p. 139)

Time for a telephone call

NB You can find the keys to the exercises on page 149 of the coursebook. You can find the audioscripts on pages 159/160.

Starter: Dealing with time wasters   5– mins

1a Phrases for managing calls 3/48   5 mins
- After students have compared their phrases in class, play ▶ 3/48 and have them repeat the phrases.

1b Managing calls 3/49–50   5+ mins
- Read out the first part of the instructions and play ▶ 3/49.
- Then play ▶ 3/50 so students can check their answers.

They do it differently   5– mins

2a Charting your day + 2b Managing your time   10 mins
- Ask questions about the graph in *2a: What does this person spend most / least of his time on? What about you?*
- Have students make their own graph and find out who spends the most time on the phone. Then find out who spends the least time on the phone and have him / her present the graph to the class.

Unit 6 Playing with English
(coursebook p. 140)

The way home
- A lighthearted way to practise vocabulary and structures from the previous unit.

Talk about it

start
finish

Tell the other player what you're going to do next weekend.

Tell the other player a piece of celebrity news you have heard.

Work in pairs. You each need a small object, like a coin or a paperclip, to mark your position on the circle. Place your markers on *start*. One of you should move clockwise, the other one should move anti-clockwise. Take turns throwing a coin. If the coin lands showing the number, move forward 2 circles. If it lands showing the picture, move forward one circle. Follow the instruction. The other player should react to what you say. The aim is to be the first to reach *finish*.

Tell the other player about your very first English lesson.

Name a reality TV show and say what you think of it.

Think of your least favourite celebrity. Ask the other player's opinion about him/her.

Ask the other player's opinion about Internet shopping.

Give your opinion on today's newspaper headlines.

Tell the other player what you would and wouldn't buy second-hand.

Say what you'll do as soon as you get home tonight.

Think of your favourite film star. Ask the other player's opinion about him/her.

Tell the other player where you might go for your next holiday.

Conversation springboards

Milestones

a) In each of these shapes, write one piece of information about yourself.

- The name of a person who influenced you.
- The age you were when you left home and got your first house or flat.
- Where you met your best friend or partner.
- The school subject which you were best (or worst) at.

- A really good – or bad – decision you made.
- Something you loved when you were a child.
- Where you spent your best holiday.
- Something which you bought that you're happy with.
- The year when something important happened to you.

b) Work in small groups. In turns, read out what you've written in one of the shapes. See if the group can guess which of the above categories it is. Then go on to talk about the topic.

Your working day

Play this game with a partner. The pictures show five stages of a typical working day, beginning in the coffee shop. Choose one topic of conversation from that stage and talk about it to your partner for about a minute. Then it's your partner's turn to choose one of the topics. Of course, you can ask each other questions. When you have each talked about a topic, move on to the next stage. The aim is to reach home (Stage 5) after enjoying conversations with the people you meet.

Stage 1 — In the coffee shop
It's early in the morning. You're in a coffee shop at the station, having coffee with your English next-door neighbour. You talk about …

… what you did last weekend.

… a colleague you like.

… something you dislike about your job.

… something you bought recently.

Stage 2 — Walking to work
You're walking from the station to work when you meet a student from your English class. You talk about …

… what you enjoy / find difficult in your English course.

… another hobby you have.

… another course you've done.

… what you know about your English teacher.

Stage 3

Lunchtime
You go to lunch in the canteen with a colleague and you talk about …

… your ideal job.

… what you'll do when you retire.

… a problem you had at work recently.

… your responsibilities at work.

Stage 4 — In the lift
In the lift, you meet your boss and talk about …

… the weather.

… a computer problem.

… the quality in the canteen.

… travelling to work.

Stage 5 — At home
At home, you speak to your best friend on the phone and you both talk about …

… what you did today

Conversation springboards

The best and the worst

- Play this game with a partner.
- Each of you needs a small marker, e.g. a coin.
- Partner A puts his / her marker on a square in the top row, e.g. *holiday* and talks for about half a minute on his / her favourite *or* least favourite holiday.
- Partner B puts his / her marker on a square in the bottom row, e.g. *colleague* and talks for about half a minute on his / her best *or* worst colleague.
- The aim is to change sides – the winner is the first one to reach the row their partner started from.
- You can move to one neighbouring square, in any direction, but not if your partner's marker is, or has been, on it.

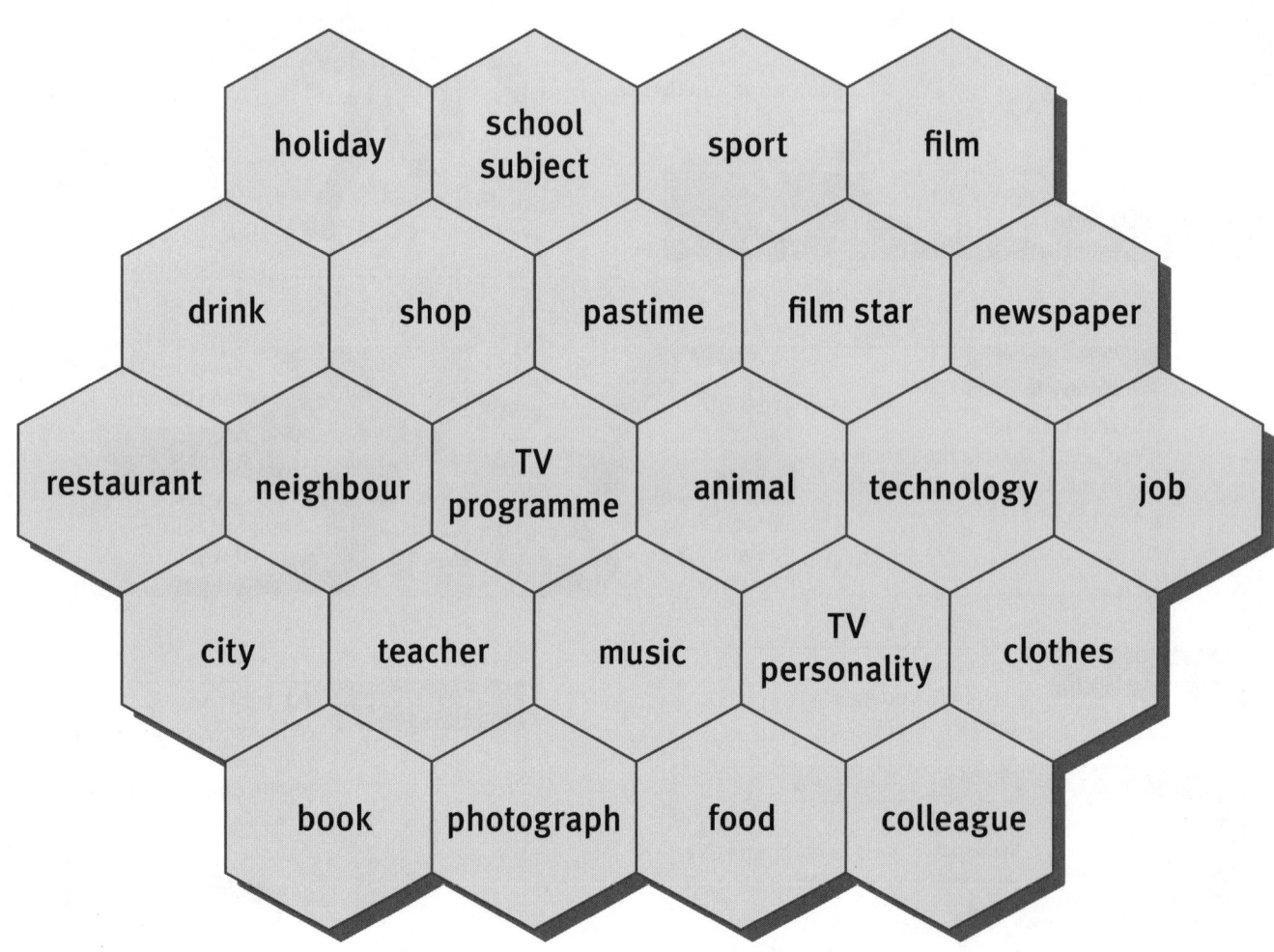

© Klett-Langenscheidt GmbH, München. Vervielfältigung zu Unterrichtszwecken gestattet.